SOUTHERN TRADITIONS

Recipes, Stories and Fine Art from the Lowcountry

PAT BRANNING

SC&G *Lifestyle*

Pat Branning

JOSEPH SULKOWSKI

SOUTHERN TRADITIONS

Recipes, Stories and Fine Art from the Lowcountry

PAT BRANNING

facebook.com/scglifestyle   instagram.com/scglifestyle

www.scglifestyle.com

Shrimp, Collards & Grits Volume III

"Southern Traditions"

Pat Branning

International Standard Book Number

978-0-9896340-8-3

Published by Branning Publishing, Inc.

www.branningpublishing.com

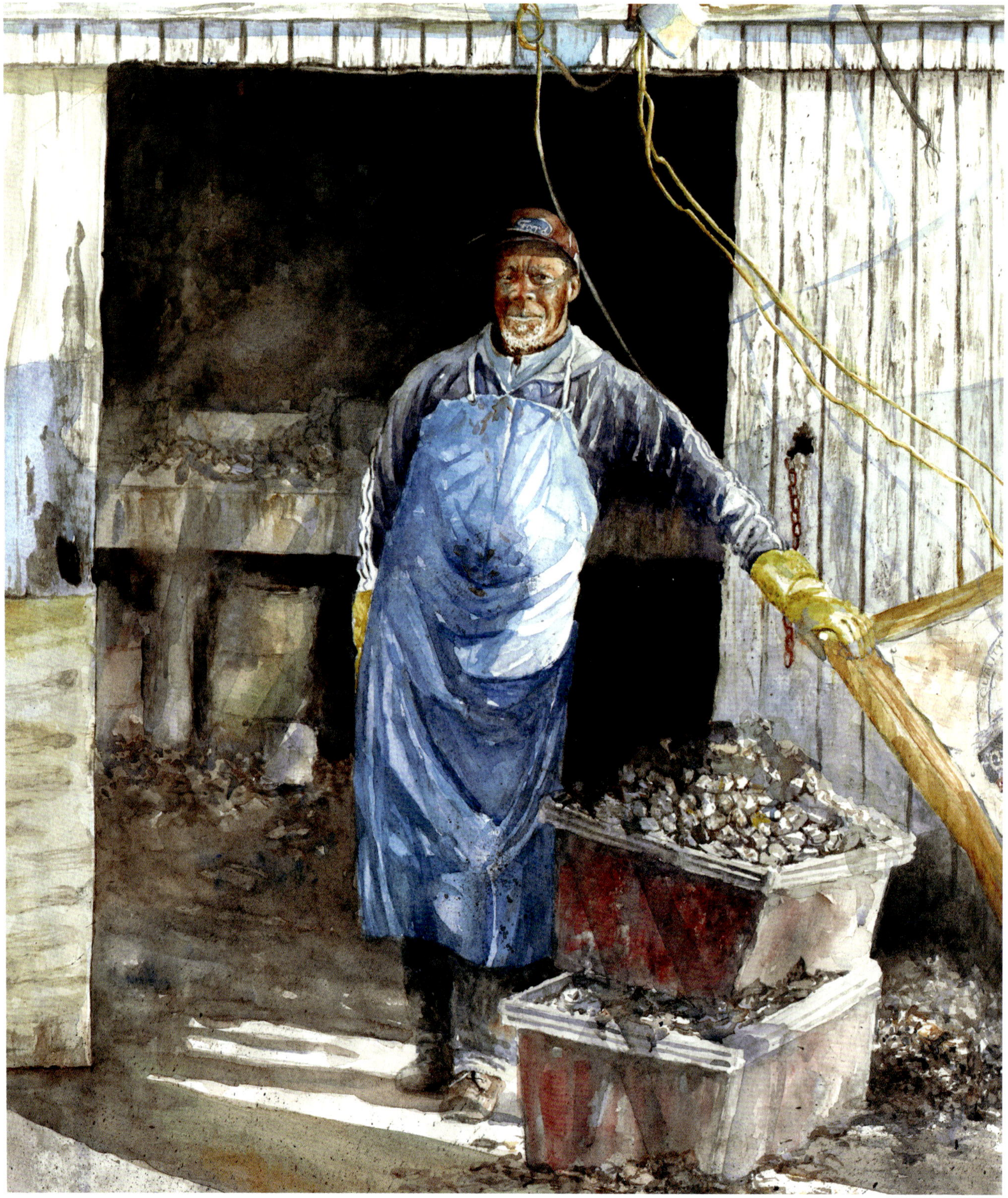

OYSTER SHUCKER BY SANDRA ROPER

DEDICATION

This book is dedicated to my family, dear friends and all others who share my love and passion for the Lowcountry.

OYSTERMAN BY MARK KELVIN HORTON

CONTENTS

Southern Traditions

Lush gardens, porches made cozy with wicker rockers and pots of geraniums, weathered docks, and scenic marshlands become settings for Southern gatherings capturing time-honored traditions and the joy of gracious entertaining. Whether you are hosting a humble backyard barbecue for a few friends and family, or a grand dinner party for ten, make it memorable.

Bringing together those we care about and adore is more than serving a meal. It's all about our greatest tradition of all, Southern hospitality.

Emphasizing creativity and natural elements, you will find inspiration for festive events and ways to create special moments in time, leaving our everyday world, and venturing into a new and magical one.

Drawing on ingredients and imagery appropriate for the seasons, this handsome collection yields a treasure trove of simple but sophisticated recipes along with tabletop and decorative accents to accompany them.

Woven throughout is a creative narrative illustrated through photography and fine art, revealing the secrets of one of the most mysterious, romantic regions of our great Southland, the Lowcountry.

My corner of the South is the land of shrimp, collards and grits – a land of gracious plenty where everyone is darlin', strangers say "hello," and someone's heart is always bein' blessed.

Welcome to the delicious world of Lowcountry cooking. With a rich history and tradition dating as far back as the founding of America itself, the food is just one part of this incredible region.

JOAN ECKHARDT

Imagine the shrimp boats of *Forrest Gump*, the plantations in *North and South*, and the antebellum mansions in *The Big Chill* and *The Prince of Tides*. These scenes and thousands more were created and filmed on a strand of mystical barrier islands along the coastlines of South Carolina, Georgia, and northern Florida. Here is where the soft cadence of Gullah natives falls gently on the ears, shorebirds soar overhead, and lighthouses guide ships into safe harbors as they have for more than 300 years.

Clusters of oysters snatched from pluff mud, roasted on a metal plate over a wood-burning fire, smothered in seawater-soaked croaker sacks, ready to be pried open. Tip its contents into your mouth for a taste of last evening's tide. Now that's Lowcountry tradition! Through simple, soulful, Southern recipes, stories, and fine art, we capture its essence.

May River oysters are close to perfection – better than any I've had anywhere. I've eaten oysters in Virginia, New York, Rhode Island and France and England but nowhere have I tasted a meaty, juicy, salty oyster to compare with our varieties here in the South Carolina Lowcountry, where they are continually washed by the flow of eight-foot tides, one of the largest on the East Coast of America.

That tide flows in and out of our vast marshlands, which are situated behind the barrier islands that run up and down the coasts of Georgia and South Carolina. The Lowcountry is an area as rich in history and culture as the land is lush.

MARILYN SIMANDLE

This region's boundaries are often debated, but the consensus is that it includes the coastal plain of South Carolina from Pawleys Island, southward to the mouth of the Altamaha River at Darien, Georgia, the colonial-era seaport southwest of Savannah. Some say it's more a state of mind than a geographical boundary. Among the early settlers here were planters who took advantage of its waters and tides and produced rice, indigo, and cotton on a scale unequaled today.

Lowcountry Gullahs and Geechees, the descendants of slaves, still cling to their patois although it has been many generations since the abolition of slavery. Isolated on the Sea Islands south of Charleston, where their ancestors had worked on plantations, their culture remained little changed until bridges to those islands were built. Today, just north of Charleston, near Mount Pleasant, a community of basket weavers still maintains the tradition of weaving sweetgrass baskets and selling them from wooden shacks along Highway 17. Once used to separate the rice from the chaff on rice plantations, they are identical to ones woven in the rice-growing regions of West Africa.

South Carolina's coast is home to one of the country's richest culinary traditions.

The Lowcountry teems with aquatic life, and for centuries local cooks have turned to the ocean, rivers, and estuaries for culinary inspiration. Crabs, shrimp, fish, and oysters form the basis of any traditional menu.

Rice, grits, and the bounty of our rich farmlands along the coastal plain also play an instrumental role in Lowcountry cooking. Whether served as a simple side or cooked with tomatoes and other vegetables to make pilau (pronounced per-low), rice is an integral part of this region's meals.

The power of food is as strong in Southern culture as it is in Italy or France. It is the strongest, most powerful part of culture and to understand a culture, you have to understand its food.

"Guess what, it ain't all fried chicken and gravy-laden biscuits," says visionary Charleston chef Sean Brock. "In fact, true Southern food is neither fatty nor simple. It's clean, complex, and, most importantly, born from the economics of survival."

Food Without Borders

Our cuisine became a melting pot reflecting the nationalities of settlers who came here seeking religious freedom when Carolina was the most religiously free place in the world, at least for a white man. Authentic Lowcountry cooking cannot be defined as either English, French, African or West Indian specifically; rather, it is the nuance of the combination of them all that makes our cuisine unique.

Charleston's chefs are increasingly going back to those old heirloom seeds and culinary traditions forged in Charleston's much younger days.

Charleston Chef Forrest Parker, who in 2016 was named South Carolina Chef Ambassador, proudly refers to himself as the chief culinary evangelist for the Lowcountry of South Carolina, with a mission to reveal the history of the Holy City through food. He reworks classic ingredients into his menus, bringing a passionate dedication to terroir (from field and the coastal waters) to the table.

Rice, food, and slavery are inextricably combined in the Lowcountry and have been since the beginning. The rice culture, not just the ingredient, was huge in Charleston and along the coast. It affected our language, our cooking, our arts, our idioms, our folktales, and how we think about ourselves, whether we are black or white.

"Stewpot cooking or one-pot cooking was more of an influence than any one ingredient," says Parker. " Think of dishes such as fish stews, gumbos, jambalaya, and pilaus.

These dishes went on to become the defining dishes of the entire South with little bits of meat strewn in. Compare them to the big roasts of meat that were standard fare in England and France. Culture. Tradition. History. For Chef Forrest Parker, these are the go-to ingredients essential for memorable Southern dining.

West African cooks also prepared greens by laying meat on top, and without that influence the Southern tradition of using smoked meats as seasoning may never have begun.

During the years prior to the Civil War, master and slave often cooked together, combining their knowledge and talents in the Lowcountry kitchens of the early 1800s. English and French recipes became seasoned by dark hands as black cooks taught their mistresses the dishes of their homeland. For example, Hoppin' John, our traditional fare eaten on New Year's Day for good luck, is what was eaten on a daily basis in West Africa.

Slave owners sent back and got seeds for what the slaves were used to eating, because they weren't used to the food here in America. Peanuts, black-eyed peas, millet, sorghum, watermelon, yams, and benne seeds all were brought here and found their way into American foodways and became part of the ingredients found in the earliest cookbooks written by Southern Americans.

It is impossible to overstate the influence rice had on the physical bearing and cultural contours of Charleston. Rice from the plantations in and around Charleston and along the coast is what made Charleston the richest city in Colonial America prior to the Civil War.

But the grandiose lifestyle of Lowcountry aristocracy came to a screeching halt with the advent of the war between the states. The culture and cuisine of Charleston was virtually brought to its knees. Nearly everything about Charleston changed, except the magnificent buildings that survived. The people stayed poor for the better part of a century. Rice cultivation was eliminated and many citizens fled to places of greater opportunity. While pride in old recipes is traditional here, unfortunately it is hard to find many dishes of local renown on the menus of our restaurants. The distinctive cookery of our affluent past may now, for the most part, only be tasted in private homes.

JAMES RICHARDS

Welcome to the Land of Shrimp, Collards and Grits

Suspended in time somewhere between Gone with the Wind *and* The Prince of Tides *lies a group of islands so steeped in history, tradition, and magical light that they stir artists to greatness and bring historians to their knees.*

Beaufort, South Carolina is a place where freshwater meets saltwater creeks, marshes, estuaries, and rivers - and all meld with the tides, sunshine, and sea breezes. Located in the heart of the Lowcountry about halfway between Charleston and Savannah, Beaufort County is made up of sixty-four islands surrounded by the abundance of the sea. These seductive islands hug the Atlantic coastline, where sultry salt breezes can feel as thick as sorghum and "haints" are as common as our time-worn shrimp boats.`

There is a stretch of road on Lady's Island, South Carolina that makes its way along the Beaufort River. The Broomfield Road passes by a white clapboard church standing in the shadows of ancient live oaks draped in Spanish moss, an elementary school, dilapidated, rusted-out tractors and farming equipment, tin-roofed shacks overgrown with jungles of pokeweed, and wooden sheds. There's a weathered brick chimney standing in an open field next to tired timbers of an old barn that groan in the breeze. A left-hand turn is marked by a baseball field - a narrow ribbon of a road that meanders along past houses painted haint blue to ward off any evil spirits. Locals whose families settled along this road years ago conduct their lives largely out of view from passers-by. Invisible to most, they are largely unchanged from generation to generation – they are the families, the descendants of slaves who were brought here to work the rice fields, pick the cotton, and harvest indigo. They are Gullah and their isolation along the Sea Islands has allowed their culture and their language to stay intact.

Soon I was to know them all by name: Miss Flowers lived without electricity or running water in a wooden hut with rotting timbers; Dora had a small blue house just outside the gate that belonged to a cousin named Harold; and then there were mighty men like Elmo who could shoot a raccoon out of a tree, bring it home for dinner, and skin it faster than anyone in Beaufort County. At the end of the Broomfield Road was Pleasant Point, about 800 acres of unspoiled, historic land with duck ponds and some of the finest quail hunting in all of South Carolina. Driving through the gates, pelicans soared overhead, while great

NANCY RICKER RHETT

white herons with five-foot wingspans flew across windswept marshlands, and egrets searched for fish in shallow waters. Towering live oaks leaned dreamily over the road, their low branches hidden by beards of gray moss. Tangled vines in the underbrush added a sinister beauty, while alligators hid out in swampy lowlands poised to capture their prey.

Arriving for the first time on the property, I noticed it was low tide and soft summer breezes stirred the pungent aroma of pluff mud. At first I thought it was obnoxious, but soon it became the nostalgic smell of a place called "home." In contrast there was the sweetness of blossoming magnolia trees, jasmine, and pittosporum. History lives here where

Yemassee Indians made their camp and six flags flew over its gentle terrain. Wars were fought, and swords drawn as men tried to prove their valor.

Rows of palmetto trees lined the Intra-coastal Waterway that meandered around the property, standing tall and majestic as shrimp boats passed by on their way to distant places. Walking up to the water's edge, we scattered marsh hens in the air and watched as a great blue heron stretched its massive wings and took flight. Standing on the bluff we looked across the river at the town of Beaufort standing like a proud Southern lady. We decided to stay.

WILLIAM MEANS RHETT, JR

JOSEPH SULKOWSKI

"The beauty of the works of Joseph Sulkowski is that his paintings have the rare gift of encouraging us to enter our own imagination and not just view the scenes as an outsider but visually participate in them. The "poetic realism" of his works takes us far beyond what is painted. If paintings are to inspire and kindle emotion, then Sulkowski's works achieve the innovative dimension of transporting us beyond the literal transcription."
- Lorian Peralta-Rmos

White-columned plantation houses still languish beneath canopies of ancient live oak trees up and down the coast. Ours sat serenely on the banks of the river; known as the Arthur Barnwell House. Never could I have imagined living in a place so full of secret stories. Behind its massive doors was a room with twenty-foot ceilings, walls lined in pecky cypress, an enormous stone fireplace, and French doors leading out into a glassed-in swimming pool. Built in the 1920s by a New York stockbroker, the word in town was that Esther Williams came to swim in this pool and the Ziegfield Folly girls arrived from New York to participate in parties and festivities that lasted for weeks at a time. Arthur Barnwell was a wealthy textile heir and New York playboy who purchased Pleasant Point and built the house exclusively for entertaining. Without bridges connecting the island to the mainland, all supplies were brought over by boat.

I loved the massive rooms of this old house - perfect for entertaining. We made friends in town and often invited them out for a gracious plenty of some of the finest cuisine in all of Beaufort. Guests could spill over onto side porches built to capture prevailing breezes and scents of tea olive and Carolina jasmine. Each spring curtains of wisteria draped from branches out front, creating a romantic ambiance.

Miss Dora came to work for us. She cleaned and cooked and made the best sweet potato cornbread and mess o' collard greens you ever tasted. When it came time for a party, she was ready - silver trays and goblets polished to perfection, her crisp white apron starched, hair done, and ready to serve with grace and grit.

A live oak stands bent over near the front entrance, so old, so massive and gnarled that its limbs are supported by steel columns. Once it had stood upright and stately during the days when the British set up their naval operations during the American Revolution. Listen quietly and you still may hear the echoes of cannon fire. Prior to that in the early 1700s, Tuscarora Jack Barnwell, an Irishman and renowned Indian fighter, had owned this land. Arthur Barnwell was Jack's descendant.

It was the 1970s and from my perspective as an Atlanta girl, time had literally stood still in this little coastal town.

I couldn't get enough of it – its people, its traditions and way of life.

Traditions are important here - I mean, very important. Immediately I felt connected to this place. I learned to drink sweet tea, feast on boiled peanuts, crack a blue crab and eat it right out of the shell. I looked forward to the dawn mist rising over the marsh as shrimp boats passed by out front and crabbers came to empty their traps. This was a time when so many small towns in Georgia, Alabama and the Carolinas all had a certain familiar look, well, at least until recently. The influx of Northerners has somehow eroded the clear edges of what being a Southern town is all about. That didn't appear to be true in Beaufort. Some might think the town looked a bit down at the heels, but I saw it as a place that had the well-worn patina of a weathered antique. The streets were dusty but shaded by large live oaks with beards of moss swaying in the wind. Traffic eased sluggishly along Bay Street and Carteret, often coming to a standstill when the old McTeer swing bridge would open for a passing sailboat or two.

A favorite spot and social center was Harry's Restaurant on Bay Street. Warm benne seed buttermilk biscuits, lightly browned, fried shrimp fresh off the docks on St. Helena Island, buttery, tender red rice with a side of collard greens, convinced me that Lowcountry cuisine was positively the finest.

The shell-pink Beaufort Inn was a gracious place for guests to stay with its secret gardens and courtyards, historic cottages and jasmine covered walls. Victorian gingerbread inns, dating back to the 1800s, represent the best of Southern hospitality.

WILLIAM MEANS RHETT, JR

Mother and Son

The Journey

Sitting at the dining table one wintry afternoon at our home in North Carolina, Andrew got up and said, "It's time for us to move back to the coast." Without any hesitation, I agreed and a little later, my husband did as well.

I will be the last person on earth to be able to explain how God works, but He was about to hand us a new road map and change our lives forever.

Shortly after we moved back to South Carolina, my first book became a success and although I had never planned on writing a second book, readers began asking when the next one would be coming out. That's when Andrew came to me and said he would be the publisher.

That was a terrifying thought. "How could he do that?" I remember thinking.

Everyone said he couldn't – so he did. Becoming a book publisher was just the first step in our journey together over the past eight years. He studied until he figured it out. Courage is the word that comes to mind when I think about the two of us taking that step into such a competitive space. Just like that, just us – no fanfare, no mentors, no fancy launch parties, no one.

Every detail had to be researched and uncovered. Where should the books be printed? There was no one to ask, so sample books began coming in from companies all over the world.

Fine art was going into each of our publications - had to be spot on, color correct. Monitors were purchased, color calibration devices and the list went on.

Andrew Branning (Pat's Son) and Pat Branning

Who's to do the photography for us? Andrew studied that, too, and bought the first camera he ever owned in his life. He's always been drawn to the wilderness areas of our coast and the whiteboot heroes, whose lack of celebrity has allowed them to go largely unnoticed as they go about their daily work. Next thing I knew, Andrew was putting on his own pair of whiteboots and heading out to the oyster flats with Craig Reaves, owner of Beaufort's Sea Eagle Market. There he came face to face with a fourth generation oysterman, Vince, who became the subject for a series of black and white images that now hang on the walls of some of the finest homes along the May River. We paid tribute to him and told his story.

The whiteboot heroes, a brotherhood of men with a passion for keeping our seafood industry alive have become the inspiration for much of our work. Every day there is a story that needs to be told through his lens and my writing. Andrew learned first-hand that watermen take a lot of risks. It's rugged and often treacherous work but there are moments when these waterways, rivers and marshlands rise up and steal your soul.

Many ideas for our stories start with a fleeting glimpse of a shrimp boat, a waterman, or a Gullah lady picking blue crab. Wherever we went, we met the South in the form of its people. When you meet the South in the form of a person, you meet a storytelling, back-slapping, authentic soul. For me, ideas for stories are more plentiful than the hours it takes to write them. I worry that I cannot get all my thoughts on paper before they are forgotten or get pushed aside for more pressing matters.

Some stories originate from back when I first lived in Beaufort on Lady's Island and have taken decades to germinate. The story of Dora who taught me how to make collard greens as pungent and salty as the marsh. She knew how to slap 'em on her arm to make the sand come out, how to salt fish to keep them over the winter, and bake fat pieces of hoop cheese into buttermilk biscuit dough – golden-brown softballs that crumble on contact. No harm would come to her. After all, her door was painted haint blue. It's Andrew's eye behind the camera that makes the unseen and the memories unfold and come to life. We both believe

LINDSAY GOODWIN

the heart and soul of our beloved Lowcountry lies in the everyday lives of ordinary people.

But we also tell the stories of the more powerful amongst us as we've traveled down Southern roads into the ACE Basin behind brick walls with iron gates onto plantations that have been owned by families for generations. Tradition runs deep in this haven for hunters, hikers, fishermen and lovers of the outdoors. In this vast unspoiled terrain, the South smells of magnolia blossoms and pluff mud; tastes like wild shrimp and coarse-ground grits; and sounds like shot gun shells at a Saturday clay shoot. Lasting friendships have been made with the people in these places, filling the unfinished corners of my heart with gratitude.

Andrew wasn't content with creating books – there was more to come. About two years ago he challenged me to start our own magazine with our unique brand of combining art with stories and recipes. Now in its second year, the challenges are great, the pitfalls are many, but the road ahead looks full of adventure and rewards. Highly acclaimed authors, photographers, designers and artists have jumped on board with us to make it all happen.

Best of all, you – our readers - have told us you like it and cannot wait for the next issue to come out. To talk with any one of you is more restorative than watching the amber and gold of our sunsets over the May River. Thank you all. I believe the best lies ahead.

You can subscribe to our magazine online at www.scglifestyle.com.

Southern Hospitality

The Heart and Soul of Southern Tradition

Chapter One

The South is a place where late afternoons beckon us to gather on porches.

Soft cushioned wicker rockers invite us to linger awhile over tall glasses of sweet tea,

and talk to neighbors passing by. Evenings are punctuated with an orchestra of

whippoorwills, tree frogs and cicadas. Tomato sandwiches on white bread slathered with

Duke's mayonnaise are the order of the day. Gentlemen wear seersucker with bow ties,

and hold doors for ladies. We love our pearls, monogram everything that sits still

long enough, cherish Grandmother's silver service, handwritten thank-you notes,

bourbon and football. Everyone is darlin', strangers say "hello" and

someone's heart is always being blessed.

Welcome to the South!

When it comes to Southern hospitality, it's not all about the fine china, sterling silver, and cut crystal. Southern hospitality isn't always fancy. It doesn't need white monogrammed linens and lace, polished antique family silver or porcelain teacups. It just needs a place where people come together and feel at home.

Nowhere was that more true than in our big backyard in Sea Pines when we lived on Hilton Head Island. There is an oak on the back of the property that stands tall and mighty, branches dripping with Spanish moss, some so heavy they nearly touched the ground. There we often gathered with our children and neighbors, celebrated birthdays, roasted oysters, hot dogs and marshmallows. There was always plenty of excitement when it came time to make the s'mores. A rope swing hung from one of the branches of that old tree, entertaining little ones while grown-ups swapped stories and gathered close to the heat of the flames.

Entertaining, whether grand or humble, is so ingrained in us as Southerners, that it has become the backbone of our great heritage and calling card of our hospitality. As Southern women the urge to entertain runs deep in our veins. The mere mention of a celebration lights a fire under us and sends us scurrying about the house polishing silver, fluffing sofa pillows, and making enough sweet tea, pimento cheese and chicken salad sandwiches to feed an army.

Southerners are famous for many traditions: gracious manners, raising the best hunting dogs, having a nose for good bourbon and speaking in a soft melodious drawl. People love what we have down here. But the main reason we are loved universally is for our greatest tradition of all, that of Southern hospitality. Our ability to tell great stories and our delicious food, lovingly prepared in our own home kitchens is part of that graciousness.

In towns and villages along the coast friends still entertain friends, gather in historic homes once occupied by the Northern army, have cocktails in parlors and on verandas built before the Revolutionary War times. And women still have double names like Mary Catherine, Sallie May or Mary Edna. Guess that's tradition, just like there always is a man named Bubba in every family, whether black or white.

Cuthbert House: a Place Where Hospitality Lives
If you haven't been there, well, bless your heart!

Beaufort, South Carolina is a place where porches are as certain as the coming and going of the tides. Standing proud on the bluffs of the river, this town so captivated me on my first visit that it led to a lifetime of trips down her sea scented streets with secret gardens, pristine nineteenth century mansions with intricate iron gates and gas-lit alleyways. Elegant porches cooled by river breezes offer respite from afternoon heat. The clip-clop sound of horses with their carriages on the streets below became a favorite memory of a place deeply rooted in history on these saltwater bluffs.

CUTHBERT HOUSE, BEAUFORT SC

War was raging throughout the South, Beaufort was spared only because General Sherman's troops had occupied the town. Rather than burn Beaufort, they turned churches and homes into offices, morgues, and hospitals. Although she was spared, her prosperity came to a sudden halt after the war. During Reconstruction, the economy was non-existent. Carpetbaggers and scalawags ravaged the town. Confederate money was hardly worth saving, and many of the grand homes were sold for taxes to Yankees, because the owners couldn't afford to pay.

While in Beaufort Experience One of South Carolina's Tastiest Traditions

As one of South Carolina's most iconic dishes, shrimp and grits is served in restaurants throughout the Palmetto State. The quaint coastal village of Habersham lies just minutes from Beaufort and reflects the relaxed pace of life in the Lowcountry. It's here at 10 Market that Executive Chef Tyler Slade puts his own unique twist on this delicacy, prepared with fresh-off-the-boat local shrimp.

In honor of *Shrimp, Collards and Grits*, he created this very special recipe, absolutely delicious with a unique way of preparing the collard greens. The recipe is in collaboration with their Chef de Cuisine Ryan Weaver, who created the collard greens for this recipe.

Throw open the screen door, inhale the scent of new blooms and let springtime in the South fill your heart with joy!

On most any afternoon, guests at the Cuthbert House Inn on Beaufort's Bay Street gather to relax and enjoy refreshments and sunsets with commanding Intra-coastal Waterway views. Nestled on the banks of the Beaufort River, the Cuthbert House Inn represents the antebellum South at its architectural and romantic best.

The house, built in the early 1800s, reflects the Federal style, and was once home to the Cuthbert family, successful rice and indigo plantation owners. It was in 1861, following the loss of the Port Royal Sound battle, that Mary Cuthbert abandoned the house to the Union Troops as she fled with her children to safety during the Great Skedaddle. Folks in town had but minutes to bury the silver in the backyard, grab a few belongings and flee to safety, often leaving food still sitting on the dining table.

During the war, the house served as a residence for Union General Rufus Saxton, whose duties included the continual and successful operation of all cotton plantations confiscated on the Sea Islands. He was responsible for managing and recruiting the newly freed slaves for the remainder of the war. Young privates who used to run messages and do errands waited in the front parlor where visitors today can see their signatures scratched into the marble of the fireplace – Beaufort's first graffiti.

A deep history lives here. Walking along Bay Street, one follows in the footsteps of bold pirates, Colonial shipbuilders, rice, cotton and indigo planters. And Union soldiers, who made this their headquarters during the Civil War.

What a privilege to be able to sit today on this porch at the Cuthbert House and reflect on the richness of its past. It so easily could have been burned down and destroyed as happened to much of our Southland. While the Civil

SHRIMP, COLLARDS & GRITS

Adapted from Executive Chef Tyler Slade, 10 Market, Habersham, Beaufort, South Carolina.

1 cup coarsely ground grits

3 cups water

2 teaspoons salt

2 cups half-and-half

2 pounds shrimp, uncooked, peeled and deveined

1 pinch cayenne

Juice of 1 lemon

1 pound andouille sausage, cut into ¼ inch slices

5 slices bacon

1 green bell pepper, chopped

1 red bell pepper, chopped

1 cup onion, chopped

1 clove garlic, minced

¼ cup butter

¼ cup all-purpose flour

1 cup chicken broth

1 tablespoon Worcestershire sauce

1 cup shredded sharp Cheddar cheese

Bring water, grits and salt to a boil in a heavy saucepan with a lid. Stir in half-and-half and simmer until grits are thickened and tender, about 25-30 minutes. Set aside on low heat to keep warm. Sprinkle shrimp with salt and cayenne pepper. Drizzle with lemon juice and set aside in a bowl. Place andouille sausage slices in a large skillet over medium heat and cook until browned, about 8 minutes. Set aside.

Cook bacon over medium-high heat until nicely browned and crisp. Keep the bacon drippings in the pan and place cooked bacon on paper towels to cool. Once cooled, crumble.

Place bell peppers, onions and garlic in the bacon drippings and cook until softened. Stir shrimp and vegetables into the andouille sausage and combine.

Melt butter in a saucepan over medium heat and stir in flour to make a smooth paste. Turn heat to low and cook gently until mixture is medium brown in color, about 10 minutes.

Pour the butter-flour mixture into the skillet with andouille sausage, shrimp and vegetables. Place the skillet over medium heat and pour in chicken broth and Worcestershire sauce, cooking until the sauce thickens and the shrimp become opaque and bright pink, about 8 minutes.

Just before serving, stir cheese into the grits until melted and grits are creamy. Serve shrimp mixture over cheese grits. Sprinkle with crumbled bacon. A unique blend of flavors makes this the perfect side dish for your shrimp and grits.

For the collard greens:

2 pounds collards

3 cups apple cider vinegar

1 cup light brown sugar

1 cup red wine

4 cups water

½ pound hickory-smoked bacon

Kosher salt to taste

10 whole garlic cloves

Combine all in a large pot and bring to a boil. Reduce to a simmer and cover. Cook for three hours. Serves: 4-5

Picnic in Style

Enjoy a Fun-filled Afternoon

Sea Pines is Hilton Head Island's original resort, spanning 5,000 sweeping oceanfront acres, including three golf courses, stables, and the famed Harbour Town shopping plaza. It's perhaps most beloved for its stunning 600-acre wildlife preserve. Trails wind for miles beneath moss-laden live oaks; bridges and boardwalks cross lakes and ponds. Deer peek around bushes, birds soar overhead and alligators swim lazily in freshwater ponds. This is where we chose to have our picnic following a day at the Heritage golf tournament.

There's nothing quite like feasting alfresco in the shade of a live oak tree to stir up a little romance or maybe just some good family fun. As a blissful day winds down, bring everyone back together for a sunset supper of family favorites. From boating with grandparents and cousins to volleyball contests and games, nothing spells fun more than a good old-fashioned picnic. Surprise the crew with a delicious spread picked up from a nearby deli. Include little personal touches like this green polka dot heirloom throw with a deep blue checked bistro tablecloth on top. Flowers from fields nearby dress up the scene: cosmos, daisies and lovely black-eyed Susans.

Hilton Head Island Heritage Golf

Celebrating 50 Years of Tradition

Plan a Spring Soirée

In 1969 Hilton Head Island was just a little-known Lowcountry treasure. So when Sea Pines developer Charles Fraser announced a PGA-level Tournament to be held at the newly created Harbour Town Golf Links over Thanksgiving weekend, people had their doubts. An unfamiliar course on a little-known island on a holiday weekend? There was no guarantee the big names would be there.

But when both Arnold Palmer and Jack Nicklaus committed to play, people began to realize that the Heritage Classic was going to be something special. And special it is, with celebrations all over the island and parties starting before the first players arrive.

For our Heritage celebration we planned an elegant soirée and moved the table to the garden. I love to have a theme when entertaining but I never like the concept of having to have a dinner party in the dining room. I prefer to use one movable dining table, sixty-inches in diameter, that will seat up to ten. This can be moved in front of the fireplace in winter, into the study, outside onto the veranda or into the garden each spring.

MURRAY SEASE

More often than not, entertaining in the South is casual—a sunset barbecue, a picnic under the shade of a centuries-old live oak, a boating expedition or a dockside potluck. But with the arrival of the PGA players each spring, entertaining on Hilton Head Island goes to a whole new level. Each April, the island comes alive with festivities in celebration of the Heritage Golf Tournament held in Harbour Town.

JIM PALMER

Garden Grandeur

Myrtle Island, Bluffton, South Carolina

As surely as tulips emerge from slumber to greet spring's glorious arrival, dining alfresco will awaken the soul.

There's something about eating outdoors that makes one's troubles melt away. Maybe it's the sun-dappled light, a cooling cross breeze, or our personal connection to nature. Dining alfresco can transport us to faraway places or remind us of picnics and parties from long ago.

Move guests around during the course of the party and just have fun. It changes up the rhythm of things to start out with cocktails and nibbles inside, then serve dinner in the garden and end up with dessert and coffee on the porch.

View entertaining as a theatrical production waiting to be designed before the play opens. Once the audience arrives, they become immersed in a world of imagination, providing a few hours of escape from everyday life. Move them from cocktails and appetizers, to dinner and finally dessert – effortlessly and gracefully.

For our Heritage-inspired soirée we have chosen an English garden with weeping, moss-laden branches creating our outdoor dining room. Layering exquisite details adds to the reverie of a long-awaited spring season. All the elements of an elegant party are here: the antique Dresden china takes on new life once moved outside in a brand new setting. Tiny Herend china floral boxes, sterling silver, and lovely glassware add charm and dimension to the setting. When these elements are set in the garden, amid flowers and dappled shade, their formality is transformed into comfortable country charm. The menu makes the most of the season's best fresh ingredients.

"I must have flowers, always, and always."

- Claude Monet

Keep arrangements on the table low enough that your guests may see across the table. Twelve inches or lower is the rule. There is one exception. Sometimes flowers are contained in a tall cylinder shaped vase well above the line of sight.

KATHY ANDERSON

RASPBERRY CHAMPAGNE SPARKLERS

Champagne

Fresh raspberries

Raspberry liqueur

Pour champagne into glasses. Add a few fresh raspberries and a heaping tablespoon Chambord Raspberry Liqueur.

QUINOA, CORN AND MINT SALAD

2 cups quinoa

Kosher salt

3 cups fresh or frozen corn kernels

1 bunch green onions, finely chopped

1 red bell pepper, finely diced

¾ cup fresh mint, chopped

1 teaspoon lemon zest

¼ cup fresh lemon juice

¼ cup extra-virgin olive oil

Freshly ground black pepper

Rinse quinoa in large sieve under cold running water. Cook quinoa in 4 cups boiling water with 2 teaspoons kosher salt for 10 to 15 minutes until almost tender. Drain and spread onto a large sheet pan and allow to cool for 15 minutes.

Combine quinoa with remaining ingredients and mix until thoroughly combined. Season with salt and pepper. Serve 6-8

DRESSED UP DEVILED EGGS

A tradition at every party!

12 eggs

4 slices Pecanwood bacon, cooked and crumbled

1 jalapeno pepper, chopped fine and seeds removed

2 green onions, chopped

3 sprigs Italian parsley, chopped fine

⅓ cup mayonnaise

¼ cup white vinegar

Kosher salt and freshly ground black pepper

2 shakes Tabasco

Hard boil eggs and allow to cool. Peel and slice in half.
In a small bowl combine the rest of the ingredients and mix thoroughly with the egg yolks. Serves 6-8

COCONUT SHRIMP WITH CARIBBEAN DIPPING SAUCE

Inspired by Charlie's L'Etoile Verte, Hilton Head Island

Oil for frying

1 cup all-purpose flour

1 tablespoon Caribbean jerk seasoning

2 large eggs

2 tablespoons water

1 ¼ cups unsweetened flaked coconut

2 pounds peeled and deveined fresh large shrimp (tails on)

1 recipe Caribbean Dipping Sauce

In a large Dutch oven, pour oil to a depth of 2 inches; heat over medium heat until oil reaches 350 degrees. Line a baking sheet with parchment paper and set aside.

In a shallow dish, combine flour and Caribbean jerk seasoning.

In a separate shallow dish, combine eggs and water; beat with a fork until well combined.

In another shallow dish, combine panko and coconut. Coat shrimp with flour mixture, shaking off excess. Dip floured shrimp in egg mixture, allowing excess to drain. Coat shrimp in panko mixture, and place on parchment paper. In Dutch oven, fry shrimp, in batches, for 1 to 2 minutes, or until golden brown. Drain on paper towels. Sprinkle with additional Caribbean jerk seasoning, if desired.

Yields about 3 dozen

Caribbean Dipping Sauce

1 tablespoon butter

2 teaspoons minced garlic

2 teaspoons grated fresh ginger

1 habanero pepper, seeded and mince

1 (18- ounce) jar orange marmalade

3 tablespoons fresh lime juice

1 tablespoon whole-grain mustard

1 teaspoon prepared horseradish

½ teaspoon salt

In a medium saucepan, melt butter over medium-high heat. Add garlic, ginger, and habanero pepper. Cook for 2 minutes, stirring constantly. Reduce heat to medium-low. Add marmalade, lime juice, mustard, horseradish, and salt. Simmer for 5 minutes, stirring frequently. Serve warm. Makes 1 ½ cups

Charlie's L'Etoile Verte Caramel Cake

Charlies L'Etoile Verte, one of Hilton Head's most popular dining spots, has been serving this cake for over 20 years. The recipe is from an old copy of the Hampton County spiral bound cookbook, a compilation of homespun recipes.

For the cake:

1 box of your favorite yellow cake mix

For the Icing:

1 stick of butter

½ box brown sugar

¼ cup of whole milk

1 tsp. pure vanilla extract

½ box powdered sugar

Cake: Prepare your favorite yellow cake from scratch or from a box. Two 8-9 inch round cakes are most suitable. You can make this a day ahead allow ample time for the cakes to completely cool. Once the cakes have set and cooled all the way, use a sharp slicing knife to cut each cake in half in order to create 4 layers.

Icing: Blend butter, brown sugar, and milk in a small saucepan over medium heat. Stirring occasionally to avoid burning, bring the mix to a rolling boil, making sure that all the sugar granules have dissolved. Remove from heat, and place in a mixing bowl.

Allow the mix to cool for a few minutes, but do not allow hardening. Beat in the powdered sugar until the icing is the consistency to spread. If the icing gets too hard, you may add canned milk to thin. Next, assemble the cake by pouring a layer of caramel icing between each thin layer of cake, and then icing the entire cake. The only real trick is to be quick before it has a chance to harden. Place in refrigerator to set.

Bridesmaid Luncheon

Grab your pearls and let's go to lunch!

Chapter Two

Southern women are different. That's a fact of life. We are taught to say "yes, ma'am" and "yes,

sir," listen more than we speak, monogram our towels, bed linens, stationery, or

anything else that sits still long enough, write thank-you notes and never

leave the house without wearing lipstick and a string of pearls.

Charleston is always a good idea! Magnificent "Sarah Bernhardt' pink peonies, ballerina-like pink poofs, with their intoxicating scent adorn our table. Displayed as either a mass of blooms or a single stem, herbaceous peonies have no equal. When it comes to weddings and the celebrations that precede them, the South could never be accused of lacking tradition.

Our alfresco table showcases peonies in all their glorious splendor, the perfect display with our luxurious MacKenzie-Childs place settings, glassware and serving pieces. Shades of raspberry, pink, and fushia highlight this beautifully appointed table. It's always extra special when you can weave in heirloom sterling silver with family china and crystal.

No brand mixes patterns quite like MacKenzie-Childs, the playful ceramics manufacturer that has graced living rooms and kitchens since 1995. And within the MacKenzie-Childs style-book, no pattern is as popular as the "Courtly Check," a glowing, almost burnt-looking black and white motif. Our delicate moss-covered purses and dainty slippers accented with pink peonies add a celebratory note to our garden theme.

For our toast we prepared Mimosas. This makes a festive drink served in our lovely glassware - so simple and at the same time decorative. Chill the glasses for a really cold and flavorful drink. Use a very good prosecco and freshly squeezed orange juice. Fill glasses half way up with orange juice and the top half with prosecco. Top off with a few fresh raspberries for added color.

Iconic Southern finger foods, never dull, intensely flavored, are always memorable and designed to be eaten in just a bite or two. Pimento cheese is one of those rich, spicy Southern hero hors d'oeuvre like deviled eggs. They are mainstays of the Southern party.

Silver trays can be arranged with elements from the outside, such as bright, shiny green leaves, cabbages, fruits of the season, flowers and plenty of candles in the evening.

Prosecco...

a sparkling white wine from Italy, pairs extremely well with our coconut crab cakes. I learned a long time ago that the very best drinks are made from superior liquors, wines, and liqueurs, as well as fresh fruit juice and garnishes. There are no good drink mixes that can compare to fresh, and no good pre-mixed bottled drinks that are better than "just made."

Just mix half prosecco and half orange juice, topped off with a fresh raspberry for a delightful mimosa.

MINT JULEP MARTINI

For our toast we prepared Mint Julep Martinis. They make martinis out of everything else, so why not out of the lauded mint julep? A hint of vanilla makes this one unique - a festive drink served in our lovely MacKenzie-Childs glassware.

7 fresh mint leaves

1 tablespoon simple syrup

2 ounces vanilla vodka

Sugar-coated mint sprigs for garnish

Add mint leaves and simple syrup to a cocktail shaker; muddle the mint to release flavor. Add the vodka and ice; shake until well combined. Strain into chilled martini glasses. Add the garnish.

Note: To coat the mint leaves in sugar, dip the sprig into a small dish of simple syrup before dredging it in superfine sugar. For the simple syrup, combine 1 cup sugar and 1 cup water in a small saucepan. Heat to a boil while stirring. Reduce heat and continue to stir until sugar dissolves. This may be stored in the refrigerator indefinitely.

"People who love to eat are
always the best people."
Julia Child

MELON AND PROSCIUTTO DI PARMA SKEWERS

1 cantaloupe or honeydew melon, cut into cubes or melon balls

12 slices Prosciutto di Parma

Blackberries

Cut each Prosciutto di Parma slice in half. On a small skewer, stack the melon and prosciutto, and blackberries alternating between the three until you have enough pieces of each to fill the skewer. repeat with remaining ingredients. Drizzle with balsamic reduction and garnish with mixed greens.

BALSAMIC REDUCTION

2 ¼ cups balsamic vinegar

Pinch of salt

1 teaspoon honey

Bring vinegar to a boil in a small heavy saucepan; reduce to a simmer, and cook until thickened and syrupy, about 15 minutes. Remove from heat and stir in honey. Cool and drizzle over plate.

RASPBERRY LEMONADE CAKE

Inspired by Signe Gardo of Signe's Heaven Bound Bakery and Café Hilton Head Island, S.C.

Lemon Curd

3 eggs

¾ cup sugar

½ cup lemon juice

¼ cup butter, cubed

1 tablespoon grated lemon peel

CAKE

1 package (3 ounces) lemon gelatin

½ cup boiling water

½ cup butter, softened

½ cup canola oil

1¾ cups sugar, divided

4 eggs

½ cup lemon juice

4 teaspoons grated lemon peel

1 teaspoon lemon extract

1 teaspoon vanilla extract

2½ cups all-purpose flour

2½ teaspoons baking powder

½ teaspoon salt

½ cup evaporated milk

¾ cup thawed lemonade concentrate

FROSTING

2 packages (3 ounces each) cream cheese, softened

6 tablespoons butter, softened

3-¾ to 4 cups confectioners' sugar

4½ teaspoons lemon juice

1-½ teaspoons grated lemon peel

¾ teaspoon vanilla extract

¾ cup seedless raspberry jam

Fresh raspberries, optional

For lemon curd: in a heavy saucepan, beat eggs and sugar. Stir in the lemon juice, butter and lemon peel. Cook and stir over medium-low heat for 15 minutes or until mixture is thickened and reaches 160°. Cool for 10 minutes. Cover and chill for 1½ hours or until thickened.

For cake: in a small bowl, dissolve gelatin in boiling water; set aside to cool.

In a large bowl, cream the butter, oil and 1½ cups sugar until light and fluffy, about 5 minutes. Add eggs, one at a time, beating well after each addition. Stir in the gelatin mixture, lemon juice, lemon peel and extracts. Combine the flour, baking powder and salt; add to the creamed mixture alternately with milk.

Pour into three greased and floured 9-in. round baking pans. Bake at 350° for 20-25 minutes or until a toothpick inserted near the center comes out clean.

In a microwave-safe bowl, combine lemonade concentrate and remaining sugar. Microwave, uncovered, on high for 2 minutes or until sugar is dissolved, stirring occasionally. Poke holes in warm cakes with a fork; pour lemonade mixture over cakes. Cool for 10 minutes before removing from pans to wire racks to cool completely.

For frosting: in a large bowl, beat cream cheese and butter until fluffy. Add the confectioners' sugar, lemon juice, lemon peel and vanilla; beat until blended.

To assemble, place one cake layer on a serving plate; spread with 6 tablespoons raspberry jam. Repeat layers. Top with remaining cake layer. Spread 1 cup frosting over sides of cake. Using a shell pastry tip and remaining frosting, pipe a shell border along top and bottom edges.

Fill center with ½ cup lemon curd. Garnish with raspberries if desired. Chill for 1 hour. Pour lemon curd on the center of the cake top and spread to edges.

SC&G Lifestyle

KATHY ANDERSON

PIMENTO CHEESE MINI SANDWICHES

Southerners are known to serve pimento cheese for every occasion. Whatever the event, you cannot go wrong with pimento cheese. We love it in our grits in the mornings, as a topper for burgers, or just as a snack. Having pimento cheese on hand is a "must" in the Southern kitchen. For our bridal luncheon we served them crust-less on a silver platter.

Yields 2 ½ cups

- 1 cup finely shredded sharp cheddar cheese
- 1 cup finely shredded sharp Vermont white cheddar cheese
- ½ -¾ cup Dukes mayonnaise
- 1 (4 ounce) jar diced pimento, drained
- ¼ teaspoon onion powder
- ¼ teaspoon garlic powder
- Pinch of cayenne pepper
- Sea salt and freshly ground black pepper
- Soft white bread

Place all ingredients except bread together in the large bowl of a mixer. Beat at medium speed, with paddle, until thoroughly combined. Season to taste with salt and pepper. Serve on crust-less white bread – cut each piece of bread into 4 square pieces.

Savannah Cheese Straws, a Southern Tradition

In Savannah and possibly the rest of the South, a party is not a party without cheese straws – the thin, crisp pastry sticks with the tang of cayenne and sharp cheddar. In the South they are always served at weddings, cocktail parties, and church socials. A true cheese straw is an ineffable combination of butter and cheese and flour that melts in your mouth and is a de rigueur addition to every Southern occasion. Making these straws is an extremely useful and extraordinarily delicious Southern tradition. Fortunately, the art of creating them is easy with instructions given by Edna Lewis, the legendary grande dame of Southern cooking.

Miss Lewis uses the simple technique of rolling out the dough and slicing off the "straws." Cheese straws improve as the flavors mellow, so make them a day before serving, if possible. A tin of cheese straws also makes an excellent gift.

1 ⅔ cups unbleached all-purpose flour

1 teaspoon salt

1 teaspoon dry mustard

¼ teaspoon cayenne pepper, or more to taste

½ cup (1 stick) unsalted butter, cut into pieces

8 ounces extra-sharp cheddar cheese, grated

2 tablespoons water

Preheat the oven to 425°F. Sift together the flour, salt, dry mustard, and cayenne pepper. Put the butter and grated cheese in a mixing bowl, and mix for several minutes, until thoroughly blended. Gradually add the dry ingredients to the butter and cheese, and mix until completely incorporated. Add the water, and mix for one minute longer.

Turn the dough onto a lightly floured surface, and knead five or six times. Roll the dough out ¼ inch thick, and cut into strips ¼ inch wide and 4-6 inches in length. Place the strips on ungreased cookie sheets ½ inch apart, and bake in the preheated oven for 12-16 minutes, until golden brown and crisp. Cool completely, and store in airtight containers.

COCONUT CRAB CAKES WITH PINEAPPLE JICAMA SALSA

Inspired by Chef Marc Collins, Circa 1886, Charleston

Yields 8 crab cakes

- 2 cups jumbo lump crabmeat
- ¼ cup shredded unsweetened coconut
- 1 egg plus 1 egg white
- 1 cup panko bread crumbs
- 1 rib celery, diced very fine
- 1 petite carrot, diced fine
- 3 scallions, sliced thin into rings
- 1 tablespoons jerk seasoning
- 3 ounces mayonnaise
- 2 teaspoons passion fruit juice
- ½ teaspoon kosher salt

Place all ingredients into a bowl and mix until well combined. Divide evenly into 8 balls, flatten into patties. Over medium heat in a sauté pan, place 3 tablespoons canola oil and place 4 of the crab cakes into the oil. Pan sear them until golden and flip to repeat this step. Once browned, repeat this for the other 4 crab cakes. Serve on a bed of creamy risotto with Pineapple Jicama Salsa.

PINEAPPLE JICAMA SALSA

Serves 4 on a bed of rice

- 2 tablespoons red onion, chopped fine
- 1 tablespoon freshly squeezed lime juice
- 1 ¼ pounds pineapple, peeled and diced fine (3 cups)
- 2 tablespoons fresh pineapple juice
- 5 ounces jicama, peeled and cut into small diced pieces (1 cup)
- 3 tablespoons cilantro, chopped fine
- 1 tablespoon light brown sugar
- 1 scallion, sliced thin

Combine red onion with the lime juice and let stand for 10 minutes. Add pineapple, pineapple juice, jicama, cilantro, brown sugar, and scallion to the bowl and toss. Serve or refrigerate overnight.

CREAMY RISOTTO

Don't fear the risotto. This creamy favorite is easy enough when you follow a few simple steps.

Serves 6

- 3 tablespoons olive oil
- 1 ½ cups Arborio rice
- 4 ½ cups chicken broth
- 1 small onion, finely chopped
- ¾ cup dry white wine
- ¼ cup butter
- kosher salt and freshly ground black pepper

In a medium saucepan, heat oil over medium heat. Sauté onion until tender, about 5 minutes. Add rice and cook, stirring, 1-2 minutes. Add wine and cook, stirring until absorbed, about 1 minute. Season with kosher salt and freshly ground black pepper.

Gently heat broth and keep warm. Add about 1 cup of warm broth to rice mixture. Cook, stirring, until absorbed. Continue adding warm broth, 1 cup at a time, stirring until most of the liquid is absorbed, about 25 minutes total. The rice should be tender and suspended in liquid with the consistency of heavy cream. Remove pan from heat. Stir in butter. Serve immediately. Risotto will continue to thicken as it sits.

Mother's Day Brunch

Glorious Spring with an Easy, Breezy Elegance

Chapter Three

"You don't have to cook fancy or complicated masterpieces – just good food from fresh ingredients." - Julia Child

Celebrate gracious hospitality by assembling striking place settings and enhancing everyday life with a little elegance and magical romance. Silver on the Southern table has long been the ultimate component needed to add graciousness. It is unequaled.

Silver on the Southern table has long been the ultimate component needed to add graciousness. It is unequaled. As Southern women, we collect china, crystal, linens, and silver from our ancestors and treasure them. We are simply great stewards of our history and time-honored traditions. I know women who become weak in the knees at the mention of Great Aunt Maggie's silver service. Why, my mother, a Southern woman through and through, always told me that any Southerner worth their grits will know multi-generational silver patterns – they'd always be on the tip of the tongue and ready for polite discussion. Well, y'all, she began giving me silver as I was growing up and from the time I was ten years old, I could count on a piece or two being under the Christmas tree and when my birthday rolled around, the same was true. It became a tradition.

Later, I became the one to inherit all the heirloom silver, simply because they all knew I loved it and would use it forever in many different ways. Inherited, purchased or given to you as a gift, no matter: bring your silver out of your sideboard, give it a quick polish and begin to use it in your everyday life. A few flowers in a silver goblet, why not? Have a silver vase you hardly ever use? Bring it into the kitchen and use it to hold wooden spoons, whisks, and soup ladles. After I lost my mother, my Aunt Lois and my Great Aunt Maggie, I discovered that to use something of theirs gave me a feeling of being connected. I use Mother's soup spoons every day, engraved with her initials, for soups, chowders and cereal, and I throw my earrings and necklaces onto a little silver tray, and serve mixed nuts to guests in one of Aunt Maggie's decorative silver bowls.

Now when it comes to parties, Southern women just "do" them. We do the flowers and do the food and carry out the execution as if it's second nature. A pitcher of sweet tea is standard fare in our refrigerators along with the pimento cheese – there just in case a neighbor or a friend drops by. I loved watching how effortless it seemed for my mother to feed friends and family after church on Sundays. She simply did what her mother did before her, always had a gracious plenty, and thus set the standard and established the tradition.

Part of living life to its fullest is making each milestone and event a true celebration. I and many of my fellow Southerners have been given the gift of a life shaped by the generations before us, those who lived and loved wholeheartedly. To have been influenced by my mother, grandmother and a multitude of Southern hosts and hostesses is a privilege. It is now my time to recognize this inheritance and celebrate life's happenings with each and every opportunity. If you haven't already, now is the time to start your own traditions.

A MOTHER'S DAY BRUNCH

Bask in the beauty of nature's resurgence, and pair splashes of silver with a palette of beloved blue and white for a porch setting that showcases the renewal of the season.

As the world around us bursts into jovial color, take advantage of the inspiration, and stage a gathering amid the breathtaking revival of life. The classic scheme of blue and white offers just the right anchor to a sunshine-filled breakfast setting while this distinctive plaid tablecloth sets the tone.

In the South, more than just food is made in the kitchen. Family and friends come together, relationships are strengthened, long-standing traditions are passed down, and new traditions are made. Once balmy weather arrives, few meals will be eaten inside, unless a wisteria-covered pergola counts.

My obsession with blue and white encompasses white china on this blue and white linen tablecloth, and all forms of blue and white china, English transfer-ware, and etched cobalt crystal and cobalt glass. For our Mother's Day celebration, we have mixed sterling silver goblets and flatware with treasured antique white porcelain. To center the eye, we have added white roses in silver cups and for the backdrop, faux miniature boxwood topiaries.

CHEWY, CHUNKY BLONDIES

If you love butterscotch, these brownies are for you. This recipe is tried, tested, and loved by anyone who ever took a bite! Fantastic served alone or with coffee ice cream.

Yields 36 bars, each roughly 2 ¼ x 1 ½ inches

2 cups all-purpose flour

¾ teaspoons baking powder

½ teaspoon baking soda

½ teaspoon salt

2 sticks unsalted butter at room temperature

1½ cups light brown sugar, packed

½ cup granulated sugar

2 large eggs

1 teaspoon pure vanilla extract

1 cup chocolate chips

1 cup Heath Toffee Bits

1 cup walnuts, coarsely chopped

1 cup sweetened shredded coconut

Take out a 9x13 inch baking pan. Place it on a baking sheet.

Beat butter until smooth and creamy. Add both sugars and beat for about 3 minutes. Add the eggs one by one, beating for 1 minute after each addition, then add the vanilla extract. Using the low speed on your mixer, add the dry ingredients, mixing just until incorporated. With a wooden spoon, mix in the nuts, chips and coconut. Scrape batter into the buttered pan and use a spatula to even the top.

Bake for 40 minutes or until a knife inserted into the center of the blondies comes out clean. The blondies should pull away from the sides of the pan a little and the top should be a nicely browned.

ULTIMATE BLOODY MARY

Makes 1 cocktail

When the temperatures drop, there's nothing more festive than greeting guests with a signature drink. The most important part of a Bloody Mary is the tomato juice. Use the highest quality you can find, preferably not from concentrate.

½ teaspoon Worcestershire sauce

¼ teaspoon soy sauce

½ teaspoon freshly grated black pepper

Dash of cayenne pepper

¼ teaspoon hot sauce

½ teaspoon horseradish

2 ounces vodka

4 ounces tomato juice

¼ lemon, cut into a small wedge

1 crab claw, 1 basil sprig and one slice bacon, cooked crispy for garnish

Fill glass with ice. Add Worcestershire, soy, black pepper, cayenne, hot sauce and horseradish to the bottom of a cocktail shaker. Fill shaker with ice and add vodka, tomato juice and juice of a lemon wedge. Shake vigorously, taste for seasoning and adjust as necessary. Strain into ice-filled glass. Garnish with crab claw, a sprig of basil and one slice of bacon, cooked crispy.

MAKE-AHEAD EGGS BENEDICT

Pure decadence is what makes eggs Benedict a star on the brunch table. Here is a very simple way to have a stress-free brunch with the Hollandaise sauce and the eggs ready to go before the guests arrive. Positively fabulous!

- 12 large eggs
- 6 English muffins, split
- 12 slices baked Virginia ham, thinly sliced
- Salt and freshly ground black pepper
- 1 tablespoon chives, sliced thin
- Smoked Salmon (optional in place of ham)

HOLLANDAISE SAUCE

- 1¼ cups unsalted butter
- 3 large egg yolks
- 2 tablespoons plus 1 teaspoon fresh lemon juice
- ¾ teaspoon kosher salt
- Pinch of cayenne pepper

This is all about the technique. Fill a large pot three-quarters full with water and bring to a slow simmer. Set up a bowl of ice water and place it next to the stove.

Working one at a time, crack egg into a fine-mesh sieve set over a small bowl and shake gently to allow the more liquid part of the egg white to pass through. Gently transfer egg to a medium bowl, being careful not to break the protective ring of egg white surrounding the yolk. This step will eliminate the thin tentacle-like strands of egg whites that form when the egg hits the hot water.

Once you have strained eggs into the bowl, gently position bowl over pot of simmering water and, one at a time, slip each egg into the pot. Cook eggs, gently encouraging each to rotate with a slotted spoon so they cook evenly, until whites are set and yolks are still runny, 3 minutes.

Transfer to ice bath and let cool. Repeat poaching process with remaining 6 eggs.

Note: eggs may be poached a day ahead and stored in an ice bath in fridge.

HOLLANDAISE SAUCE

May be done up to 1 hour ahead of serving.

Heat butter over low until melted. Set aside ¼ cup melted butter for assembly. Transfer remaining butter to a small liquid measuring cup until hollandaise is thickened, glossy, and pale yellow. Transfer to a bowl and stir in the salt. If sauce seems too thick, thin with a teaspoon of warm water, cover with plastic wrap and set in a small bowl of hot water to keep warm. Whisk until smooth before serving.

ASSEMBLY

Preheat oven to 450 degrees, and arrange muffins cut side up on a sheet tray. Brush with melted butter and toast. Divide ham among muffins and run the tray into the oven for a minute to heat the ham.

Transfer muffins to a platter. To reheat eggs, bring water to a bare simmer. Remove each egg from ice bath and lower into pot, then turn off the heat. Cook 1 minute, then drain on paper towels. Place a poached egg atop ham and add salt and pepper. Top with chives and a sprinkle of cayenne.

Note: Substitute wilted greens or smoked salmon for the baked ham for a nice change. Also, it's delicious to add sliced avocado.

JENNIFER HEYD WHARTON

Southern Blue Crabs

Always Have a Gracious Plenty - It's a Southern Thing!

Chapter Four

Culinary guru John Martin Taylor says in *Hoppin' John's Lowcountry Cooking* that the crabs of Beaufort County are the finest of the fine. "As much as I love Charleston and Edisto," he says, "something dramatic happens when you cross Port Royal Sound, a culinary boundary as real as the geographic fall line."

When April rolls around, grab your crab crackers and line your table with newspapers because it's blue crab season.

Traveling down Highway 17 south of Charleston, through vast expanses of marshlands, rivers, and estuaries, one enters a world unique and seldom experienced by those just passing through. Here is a place steeped in history, traditions, and soulful colors. Signs on both sides of the road mark centuries-old plantations with names like Twickenham, Cherokee, Clarendon, and Nemours. We turn off onto River Road and drive past Bonnie Hall, a former rice plantation built along the Combahee River in 1732. It is impossible to overstate the influence rice had on the economics of the Lowcountry. Rice from these plantations and others along the coastal plain is what made Charleston the richest city in Colonial America prior to the Civil War.

To this day no proper Lowcountry supper tastes complete without a bowl of fluffy rice. "When Mama cooked her blue crabs, she always served rice," says Chef BJ Dennis, a descendant of slaves, who embraces his people's Gullah Geechee past. "Blue crabs were a big part of my life growing up," he says. "If Mama said go get lunch, she meant, go out on the river. And it wasn't unusual to find street vendors walking around downtown Charleston peddling deviled crabs and soft shells."

"While living out on Lady's Island, it was common practice for us to catch crabs by putting chicken necks out in the sun so they'd be good and smelly. Then we'd carry them over to the docks, attach them to a line that hung from a bamboo pole and slowly let the line down. After a little while, I'd feel that crab nibble and I'd pull it up ever so slowly and then I'd take my crab net and scoop him up. I'd place all the crabs in a bushel basket and take the day's catch home where Mother would cook them. She'd spread newspapers all around the porch table and look for volunteers to pick the meat out. I think we all ate as much while we picked them as we did for dinner."

Often we'd climb aboard our boat for a trip down the waterway to Williams Seafood Restaurant near Tybee Island. They had the most wonderful seafood and their deviled crab was like no other. Here's the recipe for Deviled Crab *(Page 61)* as I remember it - absolutely the best! The restaurant later burned down and has never been rebuilt.

NANCY RICKER RHETT

At one time Williams Seafood was the king of Savannah's myriad of restaurants. Their deviled crabs were so famous that they were shipped frozen to grocery stores and supermarkets throughout the Southeast. This recipe is inspired by memories of Williams Seafood, Savannah, Georgia.

BRIAN BROWN

TED ELLIS

greased baking sheet, if you intend to make cakes. If using crab shells, place them on a baking sheet. Top each portion with the remaining ¼ cup bread crumbs. Cut the remaining 2 tablespoons butter into 10 thin pats and set on top of each portion of crab.

Bake on the middle rack for 20 minutes until the crab is browned on top. Remove and garnish with a sprinkle of parsley and a pinch of cayenne. If you have made cakes, turn each cake over revealing the nicely browned side. Then garnish with a little parsley and cayenne. Serve with lemon wedges. Yields 10 deviled crabs

DEVILED CRAB

This recipe is adapted from an old recipe book by Dorothy Harris of Adams Run, South Carolina, titled "Cooking for that Man," containing insights from the iconic Edisto Motel Restaurant, on U.S. coastal Highway 17, just south of Charleston. Before it closed its doors in the 1980s, it was known for the best deviled crab in the Lowcountry. Their secret ingredient was grated hard-boiled eggs which lightens the texture without interfering with the true flavor of the crab.

5 tablespoons unsalted butter

2 tablespoons dry sherry

1 tablespoon fresh lemon juice

½ teaspoon cayenne

1 teaspoon freshly ground black pepper

1 teaspoon kosher salt

1 large egg, lightly beaten

1 pound fresh blue crab meat, 2 parts jumbo lump and 1 part

　　claw meat

2 large hard-boiled eggs, peeled and grated into crumbles

¼ cup sweet onion, finely minced

½ cup panko bread crumbs

Fresh parsley, chopped fine for garnish

Preheat oven to 425 degrees. Melt 3 tablespoons of the butter, pour into a mixing bowl, and whisk in the sherry, lemon juice, cayenne, black pepper, and salt. Add the egg, and whisk to combine.

In a large mixing bowl, toss the crab with your hands, feeling for any missed shell pieces and remove. Toss in the grated eggs, onions, and ½ cup bread crumbs. Add the butter mixture to the crab, tossing with your hands to combine very gently, trying not to break up any of the lumps. At this point you may press the mixture into a crab cake or a metal crab shell. Scallop shells also work well. If making cakes, shape them and place in the refrigerator for an hour before cooking.

Using a ⅓ cup measure as a mold, pack the crab into 10 portions. Next, either press the patties into little metal crab shells or place onto a

PIMENTO CHEESE HUSH PUPPIES

Fabulous as an appetizer or served with a seafood supper. With homemade pimento cheese, these are sure to become your favorite hush puppies.

HUSH PUPPY BASE

- 1 cup all-purpose flour
- 1 cup fine cornmeal
- 2 scallions, minced very fine
- ½ teaspoon baking soda
- 1 teaspoon baking powder
- 2 teaspoons kosher salt
- 2 tablespoons honey
- ½ cup buttermilk
- 1 egg

PIMENTO CHEESE FOR HUSH PUPPIES

- 1 teaspoon garlic, minced
- ½ cup mayonnaise
- 2 tablespoons dill pickle juice
- 2 teaspoons Dijon mustard
- 1 teaspoon hot sauce
- 1 teaspoon each salt and freshly ground black pepper
- 1 pound grated cheddar cheese
- 4 ounces pimento, chopped

For the hush puppies, combine dry ingredients in a large bowl. In a smaller bowl, combine honey, buttermilk and egg, then stir into the dry ingredients until fully incorporated.

For the pimento cheese, combine all ingredients except the cheese and pimento. Fold into the cheese and pimento until fully incorporated.

Pour several inches of oil into a deep skillet, enough to cover the hush puppies as they fry. Heat oil to 350 degrees. In a large bowl, mix pimento cheese into hush puppy base. The mixture should be able to hold its shape. If batter is too thick, stir in more buttermilk. If it's too thin, add cornmeal to thicken. Drop mixture by tablespoons into the hot oil and fry until golden brown and crisp on the outside, 2-3 minutes.

SEAFOOD GUMBO

Recipe inspired by The Sanitary Fish Market and Restaurant, 501 Evans Street, Morehead City, N.C.. We always stopped there on family fishing trips to Morehead. Heralded as a famous "Must Stop" along the Intracoastal Waterway, it's been a tradition for over 75 years.

Serves 6

- 1 cup vegetable oil
- 1 cup all-purpose flour
- 1 ½ cups onion, chopped
- 1 cup green bell pepper, chopped
- 1 cup red bell pepper, chopped
- 1 cup celery, chopped
- 3 tablespoons garlic, minced
- 3 cups okra, chopped
- 1 ½ cups beer
- 6 cups seafood stock
- 2 tablespoon file powder
- 2 bay leaves
- 2 teaspoons Cajun seasoning
- 3 teaspoons Worcestershire sauce
- 2 teaspoon kosher salt
- 1 ½ teaspoon cayenne pepper
- 1 pound fresh shrimp, peeled and deveined
- 1 pound red snapper fillets, chopped
- 16 ounces shucked oysters
- ¼ cup fresh parsley, chopped
- Garnish with fresh chopped sweet onions

Take out a skillet and heat oil over medium heat for 5 minutes. Add flour, and stir together to form a roux, whisking constantly, about 4 to 5 minutes. Remove from heat and set aside.

Bring stock and beer to a boil in a large stockpot. Stir in the onion, bell pepper, celery, garlic, okra and roux. Stir often until softened, about 5 minutes. Bring mixture to a boil and reduce heat to medium and simmer for an hour.

Add shrimp, fish, oysters, and crabmeat. Cook 10 minutes until seafood is cooked through. Add parsley and the remainder of the ingredients, except the file powder, and serve with hot buttered rice. Garnish with chopped onion.

Add file powder after putting gumbo into individual serving bowls. Adding file into the pot will make the gumbo too thick as file powder acts as a thickening agent.

SUE STEWART

WHAT A SOFTIE!

Whether you call 'em peelers, softies, or soft-shell crabs, blue crabs that have shed their hard shells in order to grow are a sought-after seasonal luxury. The crabs' exoskeletons harden again within a few hours, making harvesting them a tricky business. While shedding tanks and closed-system production have boosted the soft-shell industry, supply still cannot meet the hot-ticket culinary demand.

COOSAWHATCHIE CRAB LOUIS SALAD

A recipe from Mother's Lady's Island bridge club. This was their favorite lunch during crab season. It's a winner anytime you can find fresh crab.

DRESSING

1 cup mayonnaise

¼ cup ketchup-based chili sauce

¼ cup minced scallions

2 tablespoons green olives, minced

1 teaspoon Worcestershire sauce

1 teaspoon horseradish

Salt and pepper to taste

CRAB SALAD

1 ½ pound jumbo lump crabmeat

Juice of ½ lemon

mixed greens

¼ cup capers

2 tomatoes, sliced into wedges

4 hard boiled eggs

For the dressing, whisk together mayonnaise, chili sauce, scallions, green olives, lemon juice, Worcestershire sauce, horseradish, and salt and pepper to taste.

Remove all shells and cartilage from crab meat and place mixed greens on 4 plates and divide the crabmeat among the plates. Garnish with capers, sprinkled over the crab meat, wedges of tomato and quartered hard-boiled eggs on the side. Finally, drizzle lemon juice over the crab followed by a generous drizzle of dressing on top. Serves 4

WILLIAM RHETT III

Easter

Served with a Gracious Plenty

Chapter Five

Delight in the tradition of this joyful day as you come together with loved ones. Plan an Easter dinner that brims with vibrant life, reflecting the
meaning of such a hope-filled occasion.

Our table is set with gold Limoges dinner plates, and Faberge Imperial Egg Salad plates. Little gifts of individual Godiva chocolates wrapped with gold bows adorn each place setting. Tiffin-Franciscan Minton gold encrusted glassware
adds to the formal feeling of the design.

Lamb is one of those nostalgic dishes for me. My mother made rack of lamb every Easter when she lived in Beaufort. It was

an amazing place for my children to visit while growing up. Their home was surrounded by acres of undeveloped woodlands,

uninhabited islands, marshlands and miles of dirt roads. After a day of taking rides on Grandpa's golf cart, searching for deer

tracks and alligators and catching blue crabs with a cane pole, a chicken neck and a bucket, we would open the door to the house and

become overwhelmed by the scent of lamb that had been slow-roasting most of the day. It tasted as good as it smelled, too. And one

thing for sure and certain - there would be a gracious plenty. Those two little words summed up her approach to any occasion.

RACK OF LAMB WITH HONEY MUSTARD GLAZE AND BALSAMIC VINEGAR REDUCTION

Sweet mustard and a tangy vinegar reduction are a tasty accent to this lovely rack of lamb. Serve this warm with Baby Peas topped with bacon and crispy leeks and Gruyere Scalloped Potatoes.

Two 1 ½ pound racks of lamb

  (8 or 9 chops per rack)

¼ cup olive oil

6 tablespoons honey mustard

1 teaspoon kosher salt

Freshly ground black pepper

¼ cup fresh rosemary, chopped

8 cloves garlic, minced

½ cup Balsamic Vinegar Reduction

Preheat oven to 450 degrees. Trim any excess fat off the bones and ribs of the lamb. Combine the olive oil, mustard, salt and pepper, rosemary, and garlic in a small bowl and mix well.

Stand the ribs up together in a roasting pan with the rib bones intertwined, fat side facing out. Brush or spoon the olive oil mixture onto the fat side of the 2 racks of lamb.

Roast for 25 to 30 minutes for medium-rare. Internal temperature should register 130 to 135 degrees. Remove the lamb from the oven, cover loosely and allow to rest about 10 minutes before slicing into individual chops. Serve with Balsamic Vinegar Reduction.

BALSAMIC VINEGAR REDUCTION

Yields: ½ cup reduction

1 shallot, minced

⅓ cup balsamic vinegar

Juice of 2 oranges

¼ cup brewed coffee

½ cup dry red wine

1 teaspoon freshly ground black pepper

1 teaspoon fresh rosemary, chopped

Place shallot in a small saucepan over medium heat until it begins to sizzle.

Immediately add the vinegar, orange juice, coffee, and wine. Increase heat to high. Boil until reduced by half, about 5 minutes.

Remove from heat and stir in the pepper and rosemary. Spoon onto the lamb chops and serve immediately.

BABY PEAS WITH BACON AND CRISPY LEEKS

A delicious vegetable to serve with your Easter feast, guaranteed to have no leftovers.

3 large leeks, white and tender green parts
    only, sliced crosswise ¼ inch thick and
    separated into rings

Vegetable oil, for frying

Salt and freshly ground black pepper

6 slices bacon

3 thyme sprigs

1 cup chicken broth

¾ cup heavy cream

3 (10-ounce) boxes frozen baby peas, thawed

1 teaspoon cornstarch mixed with 1
    tablespoon water

Wash leeks well and pat dry. In a large saucepan, heat ½ inch oil until shimmering. Add all but ½ cup of the leeks and cook over moderate heat, stirring, until golden brown, 10 to 12 minutes. Using a slotted spoon, transfer the leeks to a paper towel-lined plate. Discard the oil. Season leeks with salt and pepper.

In a large skillet, cook bacon over moderately high heat until crispy. Remove from heat once it is nicely browned. Remove from skillet and place on paper towels and allow to cool. Once cooled, crumble.

Add remaining ½ cup of leeks and the thyme to the skillet. Add a little more oil if needed. Cook over moderately low heat until the leeks have softened, about 8 minutes. Add ½ cup chicken broth and cook until it is reduced by half, about 6 more minutes. Add the heavy cream and cook over moderately high heat until it is reduced by half, about 5 minutes. Stir in the peas, the crumbled bacon and the remaining ½ cup of stock and bring to a boil. Discard the thyme sprigs. Season with salt and pepper. Add the cornstarch mixture and cook until the sauce is slightly thickened, 3 to 4 minutes. Transfer the peas to a bowl and top with the crispy leeks just before serving. **Serves 12**

GRUYERE SCALLOPED POTATOES

2 pounds russet potatoes, peeled, sliced ⅛
    inch thick

3 tablespoons butter

1 large onion

3 tablespoons fresh parsley, chopped

1 tablespoon fresh green onion tops

2 slices bacon, cooked crispy and crumbled

2 ½ cups Gruyere cheese, grated

½ cup parmesan cheese, grated

3 cups half and half

Salt and freshly ground black pepper to taste

Preheat oven to 350 degrees. Butter a 9 x 13 casserole dish with 1 ½ tablespoons butter. Layer bottom of casserole dish with ⅓ of the potato slices.

Sprinkle with salt and pepper. Layer on ½ of the sliced onions and ½ cup of the Gruyere cheese.

Add another layer with ½ the bacon and ½ the parsley and green onion tops. Sprinkle with parmesan.

Repeat by layering on ⅓ of the potato slices, and sprinkle again with salt and pepper.

Layer remaining sliced onions, ½ cup of Gruyere cheese, the remaining bacon, parsley and green onion tops. Sprinkle with parmesan.

Top casserole with remaining potato slices. Add the half and half. Dot the potatoes with the remaining butter. Cover the casserole with foil and bake for one hour. Remove from oven, remove foil and sprinkle with remaining cheese.

Return to oven for another 30 minutes until nicely browned and bubbly. **Serves 8**

KEY LIME
POUND CAKE

1 cup butter, softened

½ cup shortening

3 cups sugar

6 large eggs

3 cups all-purpose flour

½ teaspoon baking powder

⅛ teaspoon salt

1 cup milk

CAKE GLAZE

1 cup confectioners sugar

1 teaspoon pure vanilla extract

1 tablespoon lime zest

¼ cup fresh Key lime juice

Preheat oven to 325°. Beat butter and shortening at medium speed with a heavy-duty electric stand mixer until creamy. Gradually add sugar, beating at medium speed until light and fluffy. Add eggs, 1 at a time, beating just until blended after each addition.

Stir together flour, baking powder, and salt. Add to butter mixture alternately with milk, beginning and ending with flour mixture. Beat at low speed just until blended after each addition. Stir in vanilla, lime zest, and lime juice. Pour batter into a greased and floured 10-inch (12-cup) tube pan.

Bake at 325° for 1 hour and 15 minutes to 1 hour and 20 minutes or until a long wooden pick inserted in center comes out clean.

Cool in pan on a wire rack 10 to 15 minutes; remove from pan to wire rack.

Whisk together 1 cup powdered sugar, 2 tablespoons fresh Key lime juice and 1/2 teaspoon vanilla extract until smooth. Use immediately..

BEST COCONUT CAKE

Inspired by Dorie Greenspan

2 ¼ cups cake flour

1 tablespoon baking powder

½ teaspoon salt

1 ¼ cups buttermilk

4 large egg whites

1 ½ cups sugar

2 teaspoons grated lemon zest

1 stick unsalted butter, room temperature

½ teaspoon pure lemon extract

BUTTERCREAM

1 cup sugar

4 large egg whites

3 sticks unsalted butter, room temperature

¼ cup fresh lemon juice

1 teaspoon pure vanilla extract

1 cup unsweetened coconut

LEMON CURD (OR YOU MAY PURCHASE THIS IN JARS)

3 lemons

1 ½ cups sugar

¼ pound unsalted butter, room temperature

4 large eggs

½ cup lemon juice

⅛ teaspoon kosher salt

FOR THE CAKE

Preheat oven to 350 degrees. Generously grease two 9x2 inch round cake pans.

Whisk together flour, baking powder and salt.
Mix together the milk and egg whites until well combined.

In the bowl of a stand mixer fitted with the paddle attachment combine sugar and lemon zest together until the sugar is fragrant.

Turn the mixer on at medium speed and add the butter. Allow the butter and sugar to cream together for 3 minutes until light and fluffy. Add lemon extract, then a third of the flour mixture. Add in half of the milk and egg white mixture, half of the remaining dry ingredients and continue to beat on medium speed. Add remaining milk and egg white mixture until the batter is well mixed. Finally, add in the remaining dry ingredients and beat for an additional 2 minutes or until the batter is mixed well and no flour streaks remain.

Evenly distribute the batter into the baking pans.
Bake in a preheated oven for 30 minutes or until the cakes have risen and are springy to the touch. A toothpick inserted in the center should come out clean. Cool cakes for about 10 minutes. Then remove from the pans and cool for another 30 minutes.

To make the buttercream: Put egg whites and sugar over a pan of simmering water and whisk constantly for about 3 minutes. Once sugar has completely dissolved, remove the bowl from the heat. Whisk egg white mixture in a mixer on medium-high speed until it is cool. Add butter one stick at a time and beat until smooth. Add the lemon juice and vanilla extract and continue beating until the buttercream is smooth. Stir in the coconut until thoroughly combined. Set aside until you are ready to assemble the cake.

Lemon curd: Zest lemons and place in a food processor. Add sugar and pulse until the zest is superfine and is thoroughly combined with the sugar.
In the bowl of a stand mixer fitted with a paddle attachment, cream the butter on medium and add in the lemon sugar mixture. Add eggs, 1 at a time until each is completely mixed in, then add lemon juice and salt. Mix until well combined.

Transfer mixture to a saucepan and stir over low heat until mixture thickens, about 10 minutes. Transfer curd to cool, then refrigerate.

To assemble: Slice each layer horizontally in half. Place one layer cut side up on a cake platter or cardboard cake round. Add one third of the lemon curd on top, then top the curd with about one quarter of the buttercream. Repeat with two more layers. Add the last layer cut side down on top of the cake and frost the tops and sides of the cake with the rest of the buttercream.

Ruins of Old Sheldon Church

An Annual Easter Celebration —
Sort of Halfway to Heaven

FOR AS LONG AS I CAN REMEMBER, every year on the second Sunday after Easter we packed a picnic lunch and headed out to the ruins of Old Sheldon Church in Yemassee. This has been a long-standing tradition dating back to 1925 for the Parish Church of St. Helena in Beaufort to conduct an annual service on the second Sunday after Easter on these sacred grounds under the sweeping live oaks beside the tall columns. It's bring your own chairs, your own picnic and bug spray. For hundreds of worshipers, the aroma of fried chicken is a tradition in itself, along with enough potato salad, coleslaw, pound cakes, lemon meringue Pies, and chocolate cakes to feed the multitudes.

Located on a tree-shrouded byway near U.S. 21, the church was built with rice money and slave hands. Originally organized and funded in the 1740s and 1750s by William Bull, whose Newberry Plantation bordered the church grounds, the church was named Sheldon in honor of the family's ancestral home in England. Burned during the American Revolution, it was rebuilt in antebellum times. During the Civil War, General Sherman's troops burned the church a second time as part of his "March to the Sea" campaign. While the walls still refused to fall, the church was not repaired again. Later, the inside was gutted by whites and blacks who needed the materials to rebuild their homes burned by Sherman's army.

Why do folks in the Lowcountry still love to wander about these ruins? In the words of the late county coroner of Beaufort, Roger Pinckney Xi; "A visit to old Sheldon is soothing to man's troubled soul. There among the sacred ruins one feels close to the Creator. It is like being out of this world – sort of halfway to heaven. One feels as if when God made heaven and earth, He spit a little bit of heaven and it landed on a spot on earth we call Sheldon."

SANDY DIMKE

ACE BASIN

Age Old Traditions Where the Ashepoo, Combahee and Edisto Rivers Merge

Chapter Six

"The natural world is a reflection of our own inner beauty. Engaging in the sporting life brings us into intimate contact with this realization. Here, we may step away from the routine of linear time and commune with the timeless wonders of nature."

- Joseph Sulkowski

JOSEPH SULKOWSKI

JOSEPH SULKOWSKI

"The love and delight in animals is one of the truest experiences in this world. Dogs are always there, loving you, whatever you look like. They have been a part of our human lives for hundreds of years, hunting with us, protecting us and providing us with faithful companionship."

- Joseph Sulkowski

The rest of our great nation has long wanted what Southerners have. They covet our cast iron skillet fried chicken, our stone ground grits and gravy, thirst for our bourbon, gentile manners, mint juleps and cowboy boots. But there is so much more.

Due east from Highway 21, across the vast marshlands, through palmetto-studded live oak hammocks and dark-water cypress swamps, the landscape breaks into open vistas and well-tended fields in the heart of the ACE Basin's plantation country. This is the land of forgotten places, of country churches, roadside shacks, cinder block fish houses, and decades of tradition.

It's home to antebellum plantations, polo matches, fox hunting, quail and duck hunting and some of the most breathtakingly beautiful vistas in all of coastal South Carolina.

"Being outside with the horses, the dogs and all of nature is part of the thrill. It's not so much about the hunt as it is the experience, the camaraderie among hunters and tradition," says Chip Limehouse, whose family has owned Airy Hall Plantation for more than 40 years. "I love waking up on a chilly winter morning – waking up early, hearing the rumble of horse trailers arriving down the lane just as the early morning mist rises from the fields, then seeing all the hounds and the red jackets. It's a family sport – we often have three generations on the hunt at one time."

"Mother could ride a horse like a cavalryman, handle a shotgun, shoot skeet with the best of us, run the Cooper River Bridge and warm up a polo pony," said Chip. "Anytime there was a fox hunt or something going on, you could count on Mom to be right in the middle of it." He's speaking of Frankie Limehouse, the matriarch of the Limehouse family, whose legacy is one of class, honoring tradition and genuine Southern hospitality. "We call her our Steel Magnolia."

There's no doubt about her strength and resolve when one witnesses the skin of a 13-foot alligator hanging from the top of a window. Now that's a true Southern woman who can shoot a gator between the eyes and hit the mark. Frankie Fennell Limehouse, an original steel magnolia, is a true daughter of the South keeping tradition alive.

Southern Style Polo

Often Called the Sport of Kings

Traditionally this has been viewed as a masculine endeavor. It's fast, with horses reaching speeds of up to forty miles per hour, and dangerous, with spills and injuries part of the game, but deep in the ACE Basin and elsewhere there are the brave and the few willing to take it on, breaking down the sport's gender boundaries. With the first chill of autumn in the air, the thunder of horses can be heard at Airy Hall. You can bet there will be a few ladies on the field with the fortitude to play the game.

After the fox hunt, quail hunt or a polo match, participants gather around to talk about the day and enjoy a plate or two of barbecued brisket served with creamy slaw, either on a bun or plate.

AIRY HALL, SOUTH CAROLINA

JOSEPH SULKOWSKI

SLOW-COOKED COLA BARBECUED BEEF BRISKET

Serve sliced thin against the grain or shredded on a bun with creamy coleslaw. They make great little sliders for parties, can be easily cooked ahead and reheated. Top with a slice of red onion and a few pickles.

CREAMY APPLE COLESLAW

Bagged coleslaw is one of my favorite time-savers. I love the tri-color variety with shredded green cabbage, purple cabbage and carrots.

2 bags tri-color cole slaw

1 ½ cup mayonnaise

½ cup sugar

3 tablespoons cider vinegar

kosher salt and freshly ground black pepper to taste

1 Vidalia or other sweet onion, chopped

2 Granny Smith apples, peeled and sliced into julienne strips

1 teaspoon celery seed

Whisk together mayonnaise, sugar, vinegar, salt and pepper, and celery seed until thoroughly combined.

Combine all ingredients in a large bowl and toss to completely coat with the dressing. Refrigerate before serving until nice and cold.

2 tablespoons packed light brown sugar

1 tablespoon salt

1 tablespoon sweet paprika

1 teaspoon dry mustard

2 teaspoons onion powder

1 teaspoon freshly ground black pepper

1 (4 pound) beef brisket, trimmed

2 tablespoons vegetable oil

2 onions, thinly sliced

2 cups Coca-Cola (do not use diet)

1 (28 ounce) can crushed tomatoes

Combine brown sugar, salt and pepper, paprika, dry mustard and onion powder in a small bowl. Rub mixture all over brisket.

Sear brisket in a large pot on all sides over medium-heat until browned on all sides, turning with tongs. Transfer to a slow cooker. Add the 2 cups Coca-Cola and the crushed tomatoes. Place onions on top of brisket. Cover and cook on low until meat is fork-tender, 7 to 8 hours.

Transfer to a cutting board and allow to rest 20 minutes. Slice against the grain or shred. Add some crunchy onion rings for a well-rounded meal. Serves 8-10

Food created and styled by Sea Pine's Culinary Team.

ROASTED GREEN BEANS WITH LEMON, PINE NUTS AND PARMIGIANO

Courtesy of Mike Cooke and Davide Giannotti

1¼ pound fresh green beans, rinsed well, stems trimmed

1 small head garlic

¼ cup plus 2 tablespoons extra-virgin olive oil

1 ½ tablespoons finely grated lemon zest

2 tablespoons fresh lemon juice

Kosher salt and freshly ground black pepper

⅓ cup pine nuts

¼ cup coarsely grated Parmigiano-Reggiano

1 tablespoon fresh flat-leaf parsley, chopped

Position oven racks in the top and bottom thirds of the oven. Heat oven to 450 degrees.

Place the beans in a large bowl. Peel the garlic, quarter each clove and slice lengthwise. If cloves are small, halve them. Add them to the green beans. Toss the beans and garlic with ¼ cup olive oil, 1 tablespoon of the lemon zest, 1 teaspoon salt, and ½ teaspoon pepper.

Spread the beans on a rimmed baking sheet and roast in the oven for 10 minutes. Stir the beans and garlic with a spatula for more even cooking and coloring. Continue roasting until the beans and garlic pieces are lightly browned and tender throughout, another 10 to 15 minutes.

Spread pine nuts on a rimmed baking sheet and toast until just golden, about 5 minutes.

Transfer beans to a small serving platter or shallow bowl and dress with the lemon juice and the remaining 2 tablespoons olive oil. Toss gently to coat and season to taste with salt and pepper.

Sprinkle on the toasted pine nuts, the remaining ½ tablespoon lemon zest, the Parmigiano and the parsley. Serve hot or at room temperature. Serves 4-6

Duck Hunting

South Carolina Wetlands

I don't believe I ever met a man who loved the age old tradition of duck hunting more than Edward Smith of Barnwell, South Carolina. While visiting Edward and Terry Smith at their home, Cedar Hall, I noticed an unusual piece of jewelry sitting on a winged-back chair next to the fireplace. This was Edward's duck call necklace with 122 bands - evidence of all the ducks he had harvested throughout his lifetime of hunting on his plantation and others.

These small shiny aluminum bands are placed around the leg of a wild duck to gain information on migration and longevity. It is a rare thing to retrieve a banded bird and a real tribute to the hunter.

One of the best ways to warm up after the hunt is with a bowl of piping hot soup.

EDWARD SMITH'S DUCK CALLS & BANDS, BARNWELL, S.C.

TOMATO SOUP PROVENCAL

Yields 4 quarts

⅓ cup olive oil

4 leeks, rinsed, dried, and minced

3 carrots, peeled and minced

1 red onion, chopped

3 garlic cloves, minced

grated zest of one orange

1 tablespoon thyme, dried

1 teaspoon fennel seeds

1 teaspoon saffron threads (optional)

3 cans (35 ounces each) Italian plum tomatoes, undrained

12 ripe large tomatoes, seeded and diced in summer; otherwise use 2 (28 ounce) cans crushed

2 quarts chicken stock, preferably homemade

1 cup orange juice

Salt and freshly ground black pepper

1 cup chopped fresh basil

Crumbled goat cheese and croutons for garnish

Heat oil in a large stockpot over high heat. Once hot, add the carrots, onion, carrots, leeks and garlic. Stir often for about 20 minutes.

Add orange zest, thyme, fennel seeds and saffron. Cook and stir for several minutes until combined.

Add all the tomatoes, chicken stock and orange juice and stir with a wooden spoon. Simmer uncovered over medium heat for 30 minutes. Remove and cool down. Puree in batches and season to taste with salt and pepper.

Return soup to the pot and allow to simmer. Add basil just before serving. Garnish with a few croutons and goat cheese. Serve piping hot.

JOSEPH SULKOWSKI

Spotlight on Spoleto

40 Years of Blending Southern Charm with Italian Culture

Chapter Seven

Entertaining – one of the last and most wonderful rituals left in our technological, schedule-stressed lives – allows us to simply slow down and enjoy an evening. An eye-catching, beautifully adorned table allows guests to leave the world behind momentarily and escape into a realm of fantasy. Entertaining draws us together with family, friends and strangers. It's not just for those with a well-padded purse. The focus on detail applies equally to a budget-minded dinner for a few friends or an extravaganza for a large crowd.

WINE PAIRINGS

"Wine is bottled poetry." —*Robert Louis Stevenson*

A small, medieval town on a hilltop, Montefalco offers spectacular panoramic views of the Italian countryside from the tiny piazza at its summit. Although it's only a 30 minute drive from either Spoleto or Assisi, Montefalco is often missed by tourists. The walls of the town have five gates; from each one a tiny cobbled road leads, seemingly forever, up to the summit at Piazza del Commune.

The grapes that grow on the slopes of Montefalco produce Sagrantino di Montefalco, Umbria's most famous wine – a remarkable, full bodied red, high in tannins, robust in flavor, and never shy in alcohol percentage. Connoisseurs describe the tantalizing fruity flavors as "dazzling!"

It is believed the wine originated in Asia Minor from grapes brought to Montefalco by the followers of St.Francis of Assisi. Sagrantino is probably derived from the term "Sacramenti," the Christian sacrament where red wine is used.

The most highly acclaimed Sagrantino comes from Arnaldo Caprai and we recommend his Sagrantino di Montefalco DOCG 25 Anni.

The wine is aged 24 months in French oak barriques and minimum 6 months in the bottle. The aroma is complex from blackberry to rose potpourri, and from nutmeg to pepper. The taste is fresh and persuasive with an intense persistent finish.

The cuisine of the Lowcountry is a vast melting pot of nationalities who came here for religious freedom. We are a blend of the many nuances of flavors and combinations from these various regions. The supreme enjoyment of sharing dinner with friends is that the boundaries of our Lowcountry cuisine can expand to include so many imaginative culinary voyages around the world.

Every year in Charleston, there are 17 days when the city's artistic energy hits a peak with a round-the-clock menu of opera, dance, concerts, and visual arts. That time of the year, from the end of May to the beginning of June, is known as Spoleto. And it is one of America's premier performing arts festivals.

When the entire tablescape is a work of art, could the food be anything else? Every inspired offering on our menu leaves an indelible mark on the palate. Our table is set along the banks of the May River in Bluffton, South Carolina with captivating views of Myrtle Island, and is an ideal setting for revelers to sample various appetizers as they catch up at the poolside wine bar or relax on the lawn.

Eye to Detail

A welcoming palette of yellows and blues harmonizes with the stunning landscape of golden marsh grass and shimmering blue water. With a salal leaf garland as a centerpiece, the table welcomes guests with thoughtful details – artichokes, bottles of Pellegrino and petit baguettes wrapped in rosemary-accented raffia ribbon – and invites them to linger. There is no better place to savor a glorious, tranquil day than beside the salt marsh on a late spring afternoon.

Bright yellow lemons and sunflowers are a natural complement to our setting of Deruta Italian pottery, blue-handled flatware, and plaid hand towels. Hand-blown glassware balances fun with formality.

Cuisine

The recipes presented are those of Hilton Head Island resident Mike Cooke, who travels frequently to Umbria. It is here that his Italian relatives first introduced him and his wife, Barbara, to a modest wine bar called L'Alchimista, located at the summit of a small hilltop town named Montefalco. The food there is memorable but Montefalco has another gift. The gift is a wine called Sagrantino di Montefalco. Sagrantino is Umbria's most famous wine.

The cuisine of Umbria originates from its Etruscan roots, and is characteristically simple, relying heavily on seasonal ingredients that can be found growing in its rich soil, raised on local farms. The dishes recreated by Mike are traditional dishes of Umbria and have been handed down through generations and even today maintain those same principles of simplicity and freshness that originated in Etruscan times. Each one was inspired by a memorable visit to L'Alchimista in Montefalco.

PEPERONATA

Serves 4

Another simple, rustic but tasty vegetable dish.

- **3 sweet onions finely sliced**
- **2 garlic cloves, minced**
- **6 sweet peppers (2 each red, yellow and orange), finely sliced**
- **1 green pepper, finely sliced**
- **1½ teaspoons dried basil leaves**
- **¼ teaspoon dried oregano**
- **¼ cup olive oil**
- **Salt & ground pepper to taste**

In a large skillet, sauté the peppers, onions and garlic in the oil for ten minutes over medium heat. Stir in the herbs and sea salt and freshly ground pepper to taste. Cook over low to medium heat stirring occasionally until the peppers are soft and the mixture is thick, about 30 minutes. Serve on hot plates.

ZUCCHINI WITH PROSCIUTTO DI PARMA

Serves 4

A simply amazing dish with tantalizing flavors. Use a young cheese that melts easily (Pecorino, Asiago from Italy, or cheddar from the U.S.)

- **2 medium-sized zucchini sliced with a mandoline slicer**
- **4 slices prosciutto di Norcia (Umbrian) or Parma**
- **6 ounces cheese, diced**
- **1 pinch saffron threads**
- **2 tablespoons olive oil**
- **4 tablespoons chives, finely chopped**
- **4 slices of crusty Italian bread**
- **1 garlic clove**

Lightly grill the zucchini and keep warm between two plates. Melt the cheese on low heat in a 6-inch non-stick skillet, and as it is melting stir in the saffron threads. Sauté the prosciutto in the one-tablespoon of oil until lightly crisp. Toast the bread and drizzle the remaining olive oil onto it, and then rub the garlic clove over each slice. Quickly bring the ingredients together. Place the zucchini slices on hot plates, pour over the cheese, add a slice of prosciutto to each plate and garnish with chives and a piece of toast.

BARBAZZA CON SAGRANTINO AND SALVIA

16 quality bacon strips (not smoked)

12 sage leaves

3 cups Sagrantino or Rosso wine from Montefalco

1 tablespoon olive oil

Preheat the oil in a large skillet. Cook the bacon until just beginning to brown but not crispy. Add the wine and sage and cook until the wine has reduced. Immediately serve on a hot plate with unsalted crusty bread. Serves 4

CARNAROLI RICE RISOTTO

Carnaroli rice is the "king" of Italian rice and a favorite among Italian chefs. If you can't find carnaroli rice in your local grocery store, you can easily purchase it Online. Similar to arborio, carnaroli rice is medium grain, but has a higher starch content and firmer texture, which results in a risotto that's creamier and more resistant to overcooking. The grains are also slightly longer and keep their shape when stirred.

1 ½ cups rice

4 cups of hot vegetable broth

8 tablespoons butter

1 pinch saffron threads

20 asparagus tips, diced into small pieces

8 ounces fresh petite peas (use frozen if you cannot find fresh)

3 ounces Parmigiano cheese, grated

6 ounces pancetta slices, diced into small pieces

1 tablespoon olive oil

Freshly ground pepper and sea salt to taste.

Heat the oil in a large saucepan over low to medium heat. Add the rice and stir for a minute until the rice is coated and becomes opaque. Do not let it burn or brown. During this time heat the broth and keep it hot throughout the process. Add two ladles of broth and stir into the rice continually until the rice has absorbed the broth, evidenced by a clear wake occurring when you draw the spoon through the rice. Keep adding broth one ladle at a time and constantly stirring. Add the saffron threads after about ten minutes and stir them into the rice. Pre cook the asparagus and peas separately so they are ready to be

inserted into the rice near the end of the cooking process. When the rice has become creamy and has absorbed most if not all the broth that is the time to add the butter and vigorously blend it with the rice until the risotto is even creamier than before. Add the cheese and blend that into the risotto. Add freshly ground pepper to taste In a small 6-inch skillet, sauté the pancetta pieces in the oil until they are crisp and brown. Place the risotto into a hot serving dish and sprinkle the pancetta on top. Serves 4

Saffron Threads

SG&G *Lifestyle*

PRODUCE MARKET- WORKING MODEL CLARK HULINGS.

SCAFATA

Serves 4

An amazing farm-fresh Umbrian dish, best when prepared al dente. You may have to search for the fava beans, but they are well worth the trouble!

2 lbs. of Fava (broad) beans in their pods

2 lbs. of English peas in their pods

20 asparagus tips cut into small pieces

Half a small red onion finely chopped

1 to 2 cups of vegetable broth

2 tablespoons of olive oil

1 garlic clove, minced

Shuck the peas and put them in a small bowl. Shuck the fava beans and then peel off the outer skin of each bean. Put them in another bowl. Put the cut asparagus tips into a third bowl. Heat the oil in an 8-inch skillet and cook the onion until soft. Then add the garlic, being careful not to burn. Add a little vegetable broth and the peas and cook them until they have softened but are still a little firm (al dente). Keep adding a little broth during the cooking process to keep about a quarter of an inch in the bottom of the pan. Add the asparagus to the peas before the peas are finished cooking. Add the fava beans when the peas and asparagus are cooked and cook for just two more minutes. Do not overcook the fava beans, since they must be al dente. Freshly ground pepper to taste. Serve on hot plates.

AMARETTI TORTA

Serves 10

Umbria produces a wealth of fresh produce, including almonds.

20 amaretti cookies (for the Torta mix)

8 amaretti cookies (for the topping)

1 cup of sugar

1 cup (2 sticks) of unsalted butter at room temperature

½ cup of semi-sweet chocolate chips

5 large eggs, separated

2 tablespoons Grand Marnier

½ cup all-purpose flour

¼ cup orange marmalade

Preheat the oven to 350ºF. Grease a 9- or 10-inch cake pan and line the bottom with a circle of parchment paper.

Blend the 20 amaretti cookies and chocolate chips in a food processor until finely chopped. Using an electric mixer, cream together the sugar and butter until pale yellow, about 2 minutes. Add the egg yolks one at a time, incorporating each yolk before adding the next. Once all five are added, continue to cream the mixture until light and fluffy, about 4 minutes. Add the Grand Marnier. With the mixer on low, add the flour and then the chocolate and amaretti mixture until fully blended.

In a medium bowl, whip the egg whites until peaks form, about 3 to 4 minutes. Add one third of the egg whites into the mixture on low speed. Then gently fold in the remaining egg whites by hand. Pour the mixture into the pan and bake for 45 to 50 minutes (or until a toothpick can be inserted in the center and come out clean). Allow to cool for 10 minutes. To remove the cake, flip the pan onto a platter and gently remove. Cool to room temperature.

Spread orange marmalade over the top and sprinkle the 8 crushed amaretti cookies on top.

Whiteboot Heroes

A Brotherhood of Men with a Passion to Keep Our Seafood Industry Alive

Chapter Eight

The term "whiteboot" is used throughout the brotherhood of fisherman all over the world. Coined from the use of rubber whiteboots to keep their feet dry and protected whether on the deck of a shrimp boat, crab boat or walking on oyster beds.

OPPOSITE PAGE: Prints of this painting will be sold to honor the women and other workers and help fund a new foundation Fraser has endowed to preserve the waterways and prolong the sustainable harvest of seafood. Helena Fox Fine Arts, Charleston, South Carolina.

Bluffton Oyster Factory Shuckers by West Fraser

Oyster *Farming*

St. Helena Island, S.C.

Craig Reaves of Sea Eagle Market emptying oyster cages on his oyster farm.

These pure-in-their-purpose wooden vessels, perfect in form and function, were the rough-hewn, wide-planked, shallow-draft beauties of the Carolina waterways.

A s soon as you arrive in Charleston, you know you are in a special place with its own unique style of Southern coastal charm. Oyster bar dining comes with breathtaking ocean views, local live music, shady courtyard seating, and salty autumn breezes. And in backyards from McClellanville, South Carolina, to Murrells Inlet and down through Jekyll Island to Jacksonville, with the first chill of autumn, oysters get smoked in their shells over smoldering oak and hickory wood, resulting in an incredible taste.

The World is His Oyster – Year-Round

When I met up with Frank Roberts down in South Carolina's ACE Basin, he had plenty to tell us about the South Carolina coast fast becoming the Napa Valley of oysters. "Oysters are the sea's version of fine wine; their taste varies with the water they grow in. Just like the chardonnays of California, each oyster is expressive of the locale where it is raised." Currently, there is an oyster renaissance underway in the creeks and rivers of the southeastern United States, from Virginia all the way down to Florida's Apalachicola Bay. Meanwhile in the vast waterways of the Coosaw, Frank Roberts has developed an oyster for year-round enjoyment.

Red Bluff Plantation

Sporting Traditions Abound on the Plantations of S.C.

Sporting traditions, conservation and history abound on the plantations of South Carolina.

As we drove through the iron gates we entered sweet-smelling pinelands. Woodpeckers were noisily calling and hammering on trees while bluebirds flew overhead. The meeting of land and river as well as saltwater and freshwater creates a particularly vibrant niche for wildlife. High in the dreamy towering pines a cool wind murmured. All life seemed contented here.

Now we were on over six thousand acres of forest land, owned by American Timberlands, located between the Wright River and the New River just minutes north of historic downtown Savannah, Georgia. In the distance were views of the white clapboard main house just ahead, and across the river Daufuskie Island and Palmetto Bluff. This is quail country. But on this particular evening we were here for a Lowcountry oyster roast and dinner. As is often the case in the Deep South, the weather was mild, but comfortable enough to build a roaring fire for roasting oysters beneath a canopy of pine and live oaks. At the communal table, often a piece of plywood ½-inch thick on sawhorses, everyone can find a common ground. With each shovelful, each cluster, there's a sense of living in the present that seems to bring everyone together. We're all in this, and would you pass the hot sauce, please?

Nestled between the New River and the Wright River, Red Bluff is just 11 miles north of historic Savannah, Georgia.

INSIDE THE BARN AT RED BLUFF PLANTATION.

INSIDE THE BARN AT RED BLUFF PLANTATION.

MIGNONETTE SAUCE

A perfect sauce for oysters on the half-shell

Yields: about ⅔ cup

½ cup white wine vinegar

½ teaspoon onion, grated

½ teaspoon freshly squeezed lemon juice

3 teaspoons shallots, minced

2 teaspoons chives, minced

A pinch or two of parsley, minced

Kosher salt and freshly ground black pepper

Combine all ingredients in a Mason jar and shake vigorously to combine. Chill several hours before serving as a dipping sauce for roasted oysters.

SANDY DIMKE

CLASSIC LOWCOUNTRY OYSTER STEW

This recipe is from friends of the Beaufort Yacht and Sailing Club, Beaufort, South Carolina Ridiculously simple. That's the beauty of it. It's so pure.

Serves 6-8

¼ cup butter

½ cup celery, minced fine

⅓ cup shallots, minced fine

1 cup liquor from freshly shucked oysters or bottled clam juice

3 cups whole milk

3 cups heavy cream or half and half

¼ teaspoon Worcestershire sauce

¼ teaspoon Tabasco sauce

¼ teaspoon salt

1 quart shucked oysters

½ cup parsley, finely chopped

Freshly ground black pepper

Melt ¼ cup butter in a saucepan over medium heat. Add celery and shallot, and sauté until softened. Add oyster liquor or clam juice, milk, cream or half and half, and bring to a gentle simmer. Stir in Worcestershire sauce, Tabasco, and salt.

Add oysters to the base and poach for about two minutes. Remove with a slotted spoon, dividing the oysters between warmed serving bowls.

Just before serving, bring stew to a boil over high heat and ladle the soup over the oysters.

Sprinkle fresh parsley and a generous grind of pepper into each bowl. Serve with crunchy oyster crackers.

LINDSAY GOODWIN

MICHAEL HARRELL

FRIED OYSTERS

1 pint oysters

1 to 2 cups all-purpose flour

1 egg

½ cup whole milk

3-4 cups cracker meal

Vegetable oil for frying

Drain oysters and pat dry with paper towels. Place each oyster in the flour, then in the egg which has been beaten with the milk, and then in the cracker meal. Place oysters on a cookie sheet in a single layer and refrigerate for 1 hour. Bring oil to boiling point in a deep fryer. Place oysters in a single layer in fryer basket. Cook several minutes and drain on paper towels. Serve hot. Serves 4

ROASTED CHESTNUT AND OYSTER DRESSING

Recipe inspired by my father who grew up on the Chesapeake Bay in Virginia. Every Thanksgiving he and Mother sat around the kitchen table peeling and chopping roasted oysters for this delicious dressing. Warm, briny oysters and the earthy sweetness of the chestnuts combine to create a delicious balance of saltiness and sweetness. A perfect side dish to serve with Cornish hens, chicken or any kind of poultry for a special supper.

12 cups unsweetened cornbread, cut into ½ inch cubes and

toasted

¾ cup unsalted butter, melted

5 tablespoons unsalted butter

2 cups onions, chopped

1 ½ cups celery, chopped

2 cloves garlic, finely minced

1 pound breakfast sausage, casings removed

2 tablespoons fresh sage, chopped fine

2 teaspoons fresh thyme

1 ½ teaspoons sea salt

Freshly ground black pepper

½ teaspoon ground nutmeg

1 pint freshly shucked oysters, roughly chopped and liquor

reserved

1 cup chicken broth

¾ cup milk

3 large eggs, lightly beaten

3 teaspoons unsalted butter

1 ½ dozen roasted chestnuts, peeled and roughly chopped

Heat oven to 400 degrees. Toss cornbread cubes with melted butter and lay out flat on a baking sheet. Bake, stirring several times, for 30 minutes or until nicely browned.

Melt 5 tablespoons butter in a large skillet over low to moderate heat. Sauté onions, celery, and garlic until softened, about 6 minutes. Transfer cooked vegetables to a large bowl and add the toasted cornbread, tossing gently to combine. Cook the sausage and add it to the cornbread mixture. Stir in herbs and spices and the oysters with reserved oyster liquor. Mix gently with a wooden spoon.

Transfer into a large pot. Add chicken broth and milk together and bring to a gentle simmer. Pour over dressing mixture and fold in. Next, fold in the lightly beaten eggs.

Butter a 9x13 baking dish, add the oyster and cornbread mixture, dot with butter, and sprinkle chestnuts over the top. Do not pack down the mixture. It should be placed loosely in the pan.

Turn oven to 350 degrees and bake the casserole until nicely browned, about 30 minutes. Cover with foil for the first half of the baking time. Serve hot. Serves 6-8

Beaufort's Mountain Vanished Forever

Gone with the Tides of Time and Change

Remembrances of Nancy Ricker Rhett

Imagine a place with no gasoline engines and no traffic troubles, where a fellow could ride his horse from Bluffton to Buckingham Landing to catch a bateau to Hilton Head Island without seeing another person along the way. Without jet skis and high-powered motor boats, he could travel silently through the creeks and sounds, relying on the tide and the wind to help power his oars or sails. He might even hear the mullet jumping and the "whoosh" of a dolphin passing by.

In 1900, all of Beaufort County had a population of only 35,000. With no theaters or other forms of entertainment, the men and women of this era became skilled storytellers. Crabs were so plentiful, they said, on a summer afternoon, even a child could walk along the creek's edge with one stout stick, and throw dozens of them onto the bank, hook them with their back fins around a second stick and bring Mama enough crabs for Sunday supper. They told other stories of how Hilton Head Island became famous for butter beans, how Daufuskie built its reputation on its liquor stills, and how the oyster-shell streets of Bluffton filled up with people several times a week when the important passenger and cargo steamers tied up to the dock at the end of Calhoun Street.

Then along came the developers and with them, dollars whipping through the area and transforming much of the natural landscape. Everything is, as the Gullahs say, "all change up." And yet it is possible to go back to a slower and quieter era through the memories of men and women who lived here and watched the change. Artist Nancy Ricker Rhett has lived in Beaufort for most of her life and has seen the changes first hand.

"Once upon a time there was a mountain along the river on Lady's Island, a big white mountain you could see from the Beaufort bridge. It would come and go as the seasons cycled, rising and falling as if with the tide. It was entirely made of oyster shells, bleached white, waiting to be planted. This was the site of Beaufort's oyster factory, built in 1904 by Gilbert Maggionni and was part of an extensive series of his family's canning operations that ranged from Yonges Island south of Charleston down the coast to Savannah. The employees were Gullahs, the local indigenous blacks, descendants of freed slaves who remained on nearby islands," says Nancy.

Maggioni had established his first cannery on Daufuskie Island in 1893 before opening others. These canneries were among the 16 oyster factories in operation in South Carolina between 1893 and 1905.

At the close of the century, many Gullah people farmed their own small plots, producing vegetables for local markets and supplementing their diet and income by oystering and fishing.

During fall and winter, Gullah men went out in flat-bottomed boats called bateaux, pronounced "battoes." made of pine or cypress planking, or in larger sloops or engine-powered scows, from which they used short-handled "grabs" to harvest oysters from the riverbanks. In deep water, they used long-handled tongs. One man could gather 60 to 100 bushels during a low tide. They then transported them to nearby landings, loaded them onto pickup trucks, and then they were driven to the factory to be steamed and shucked and canned. Sea Island women, and often the children, worked long hours in shucking houses. "For protection, the oysters were covered with wet croaker sacks while being transported.

NANCY RICKER RHETT

Backbreaking, hard work but an honest wage after all," remembers Nancy.

In the cold of winter, a smudge pot might be used, a metal drum snuggled on a pad of sand in the bottom of the boat to prevent a fire. Clever, necessary, but a hazard nonetheless. The fire's warming glow would illuminate faces often including a wife who'd tend to the stoking as well as the grabbing.

"Back at the factory, the boiler would be lit before daybreak, ready to operate the works. Oysters, offloaded from the trucks, would be put on lumbering conveyor belts traveling through the plant to begin the process. Back in those days, the oysters were opened by running them through steam chests. The canning was a complicated system of conveyor belts, huge steam vats, cooking and washing processes, and rotating drums that knocked the steamed shells open. The meat was separated from the shells and went on to be inspected by Gullah women on each side of another conveyor belt, and then on to be canned and shipped out nationally. The shells themselves traveled in a different direction. And it was these shells that formed the mountain I grew up seeing," says Nancy.

Each year the mountain was loaded back onto barges by a drag-line, and hauled by tugboats and barges back to the shoreline where they had been found. Here they were planted to provide a substrate for oyster larvae to settle. Parched white shells were blown overboard by huge water jets, scattering them into the creeks. They would grow the spats that eventually became new oysters and the cycle would repeat.

Eventually this entire operation became a dinosaur. A slow decline began as less rugged jobs could be found elsewhere and foreign competition hurt the market. The plant was torn down in the 1970s, the docks pulled up, and the dry dock and railway were dismantled. The end

had come. Property was just too valuable to sit empty, so along came the developers. Today there is not a trace of the hectic activities that once defined a colorful, honored, and grand industry.

Somewhere in the late 1970s and early 1980s, the bateaux were beached, the shucking houses and canneries closed, with only a few photographs remaining as a reminder of a vital element in the cultural history of the South.

Yet if you listen carefully it's still possible to hear the squawk of blue herons overhead, and the rattle of wind in palmettos and from certain vantage points, watch the tide come and go twice a day.

Today Beaufort's bounty remains in our creeks and rivers, but the big white mountain is just a memory – vanished with the tides of time and change.

MICHAEL HARRELL

MICHAEL HARRELL

Champagne & Oysters

Festive Ideas for Autumn Entertaining

Plan an autumn backyard gathering featuring oysters. Here we dress it up with vintage oyster plates and a gorgeous mandala tapestry tablecloth. The magic is in the details.

Autumn in the South is a quiet interlude when our landscape changes from verdant greens to vibrant yellows, reds, and oranges. Our marsh grass takes on a golden glow as the sweltering summer sun cools down and winter is yet to unveil its chilly grasp – a beautiful time of year to gather around with friends and enjoy the best of the season.

Keep it simple, but create a little magic with just a spoonful of imagination, a dash of time and a few dollops of courage. Our garden table is set with gold chargers and lovely Italian glass hand-painted plates topped with gold-trimmed vintage oyster plates, perfect for serving Oysters Rockefeller. Oyster shells, hand painted gold, serve as individual salt and pepper dishes provided at each place setting. Bamboo serving ware, leopard candlesticks, antique green glasses with hand-painted Champagne flutes, and a tropical arrangement in a vintage green

vase sit on top of a gorgeous mandala tapestry tablecloth.

For those who love vintage china and dinnerware, these oyster plates are treasures from the past worth holding onto. They've been around for a longtime, dating back to the Victorian Era, when serving oysters on the half shell first became a delicacy.

Because oyster shells are heavy and could easily scratch delicate china, the oyster plates were used to serve the oysters without the shell while maintaining the stylish half shell appearance.

THE BEAUTY OF VINTAGE OYSTER PLATES

HENRY'S CHEESE SPREAD

Inspired by Henry's on Market Street, Charleston

10 ounces extra sharp cheddar cheese, grated

2 ounces lager or ale

Juice of 1 lemon

2 tablespoons Worcestershire sauce

1 tablespoon horseradish, drained

2 teaspoons Tabasco sauce

1½ teaspoons dry mustard

1 garlic clove, minced

1 teaspoon chives, chopped

Combine all ingredients in the bowl of a food processor and pulse until the mixture is smooth and spreadable. Transfer to a decorative bowl and serve with your favorite crackers, carrot sticks or celery.

Shrimping

Tradition as Old as the Lowcountry Itself

Among the wreckage of a once-glorious fleet, there are still those brave souls with the dignity and strength to keep the local industry alive. Most any afternoon in Beaufort is a perfect time to ride out to St. Helena Island to purchase shrimp and blue crab fresh from the weathered docks at Village Creek. Where pavement turns into a narrow two lane dirt road off highway 21, the once shuttered Dopson Seafood House on Factory Creek is now home to a vibrant seafood destination, the vision of Captain Craig Reaves, a fourth generation waterman. What was once a ramshackle wooden walkway, now rebuilt, stretches toward the floodlights of a shrimp trawler named the *Gracie Belle*. Beside her is the *Carolina Pride*. Her tangle of furled nets, steel winches, chains, and ropes reach into the sky. Water laps the docks as young men ready the boats to leave. In an industry dominated by old salts, some of whom have been trawling shrimp for more than fifty years, Craig's brother, Cameron Reaves, and his crew are remarkable for their youth. He is captain of the *Carolina Pride*.

On any given day the quiet solitude of the creek and surrounding marsh are quickly shattered as the *Carolina Pride*'s and the *Gracie Belle*'s engines start up. Each morning during shrimp season they make their way before dawn through dark waterways to the open sea, leaving behind the scent of diesel fumes and strong, fresh-brewed coffee.

Exiting the creek may be the trickiest part with its invisibly shifting sandy bottom. Once at sea it's all hands on deck. With the breaking dawn, working silently but swiftly with precision, the men unfurl nets, lower outrigger booms, and position the wide trawl net to drag roughly twenty feet below along the ocean floor. The wide mesh will scoop up everything in its path for the next few hours, its filter spitting out anything wider than three inches, a device developed to protect sea turtles. The sea rolls black and eerie as the nets are tossed over the sides.

Anticipation is huge as the nets are finally pulled from the sea and contents spilled onto the deck. Immediately workers, called strikers, pull up on small wooden stools to begin culling and heading the shrimp. It's a sight to behold as sea gulls swarm above screeching and feasting. Nets are dropped several times over the course of the day. The aroma of frying bacon, sausage and shrimp burgers is ever present as the crew prepares its mid-day meal. As evening approaches, nets are dropped and hauled one last time with the captain and crew hopeful for that one big catch.

If you park under the sprawling live oak overlooking the river, you'll be able to watch the shrimp boats, draped with their sea-green nets, arriving at the docks.

In the 1960s Richard Gay, one of the owners of Gay Seafood Company, also on St. Helena Island, was credited with being the first to create Frogmore Stew. Also known as Lowcountry Boil, it is a tradition here in the

SANDRA ROPER

Lowcountry and has been bringing friends and families together for generations. Actually the origin of this meal goes even farther back to the cuisine of the Gullah/Geechee peoples of the Sea Islands along the coasts of Georgia and South Carolina. African slaves brought with them cooking influences from their homeland – things like one-pot cooking.

SHRIMP AND CORN FRITTERS
Recipe by Chef Tyler Slade, 10 Market, Beaufort, S.C.

2 cups cooked shrimp, chopped small

2 cups corn, divided

½ cup cornmeal

1 bell pepper, minced

1 white onion, minced

1 whole egg, beaten

2 tablespoons white sugar

2 teaspoons salt

½ teaspoon black pepper

½ cup all-purpose flour

3 tablespoons parsley, chopped fine

4 whipped egg whites

Vegetable oil

In a food processor combine 1 ½ cups corn, cornmeal, onion, salt and the whole egg. Beat until it forms a wet-looking batter. Remove mixture from processor and place in mixing bowl. In a separate mixing bowl, whisk egg whites to medium peaks. Fold egg whites and remaining ingredients into the corn batter. Pour oil into skillet about half up the sides. Allow batter to rest while the oil is getting hot.

Carefully drop mounded spoonfuls of batter into the 350 degree oil. Cook until golden brown, turning once to brown the other side, if necessary. Remove fritters to paper towels to cool.

FROGMORE STEW

Frogmore stew is named for a former tiny town on the coastal island of St. Helena. It's been a Lowcountry tradition at parties and celebrations for generations and is often served outdoors on newspaper-covered picnic tables, with frosty mugs of ice-cold beer.

4 quarts cold water

¼ cup Old Bay seasoning

1 tablespoon kosher salt

4 celery stalks, cut into 1-inch pieces

1 yellow onion, diced

1 garlic head, halved crosswise

1 ½ pounds small red potatoes

4 ears of corn, shucked, each cut into 4 pieces

2 pounds smoked sausage, cut into 1 ½ inch slices

2 pounds shrimp, deveined and in the shell

2 pounds blue crab, cleaned and prepared

In a large stockpot over medium-high heat, combine the water, Old Bay seasoning, the salt, celery, onion, garlic and potatoes and bring to a boil.

Reduce the heat to medium-low and simmer until the potatoes are tender when pierced, 10 to 20 minutes.

Add the corn and sausage to the pot and simmer until the corn is tender, 4 to 5 minutes. Toss in the cleaned and prepared blue crabs and start to cook.

After about 4 minutes, toss in the shrimp and continue to simmer crabs and shrimp together for another 4 minutes. Taste the broth and adjust the seasonings with salt.

Transfer the stew to a large soup tureen or serving bowl and serve at once. Or toss it on the picnic table lined with newspapers.

Pitchforking for Flounder on the Barrier Islands

Illustrated by Bluffton artist Doug Corkern

BETWEEN ST. HELENA SOUND and Port Royal Sound, lying along the South Carolina coast a short distance from Beaufort, are eight barrier islands. Two miles north of these jewels is the southern shoreline of St. Helena Island. It was on this island at water's edge that legendary sportsman and Lowcountry native Pierre McGowan grew up. His father, Sam, was the rural mail carrier for St. Helena and he had no problem letting his young sons navigate deep rivers alone, day or night, but no doubt his mother endured many sleepless nights in their absences.

For nearly 80 years, Pierre McGowan has been fishing and hunting amongst these rivers and tidal creeks. "Spending money was scarce during the Great Depression, and I was always looking for ways to come up with a little extra cash," says Pierre. "The easiest way for us to make a few extra dollars came from the creeks out in front of our house on St. Helena."

Pitchforking for Flounder

Vast oyster beds were located in front of Pierre's house that intertwined with numerous small creeks at low tide. This area extends east toward Coffin Point for about five miles and varies in width from several hundred yards to as much as a mile. Historically the area has been called the Harbor River Flats. At low tide, the creeks separating the oyster beds provide refuge for the flounder. Having filled his stomach with finger-length mullet, the flounder buries into the mud and silt at the bottoms of these creeks to await flood tide. Pierre said, "When the tide is ebbing, the water in these creeks is muddy and the unwary flounder is unable to detect the approaching predator — a two-legged one holding a pitchfork in his hand."

This method of fishing is called pitchforking and was probably introduced or started in estuaries along the coast during slavery times and passed down from one generation to another. "It was taught to my brothers and me when we were young teenagers by older black friends and was an easy way to catch flounder," says Pierre. "Often it was our way to put a meal on the table. It's a

method where the fisherman walks through the muddy water sticking the pitchfork into the bottom in front of him, blind gigging. A gig is a fish spear usually of five prongs mounted on a sturdy lightweight pole and the darker the night the better. Back in the '40s we used gas lanterns to light the way."

When the fisherman feels a quiver coming from the end of the pitchfork, he knows he has caught either a flounder or a stingray. Since the pitchfork has no barbs, when the fish is lifted out of the water, its wiggling can cause it to slip off and escape. Therefore the fisherman must carefully ease several fingers into the gills and while holding it securely, raise the fish and the pitchfork out of the water at the same time. Next the fish is placed on a stringer, one end of which is secured to his belt.

"On many Friday nights my two brothers and I would leave the house at dark, returning home at two o'clock on Saturday morning with seventy-five to a hundred flounder. We were selective about where we peddled our fish. We sold them door to door only in 'The Point,' Beaufort's most exclusive neighborhood," says Pierre. "Word traveled fast, and it didn't take long before residents would be waiting at the sidewalk, usually with a metal dishpan in hand. A five-pound flounder would bring fifty cents. In about two hours our catch would be gone and three very happy boys then made their way home."

This is a sport still participated in today in the creeks and rivers of the Lowcountry by natives and newcomers alike.

Sunday Supper in the South

It's a Tradition!

Chapter Nine

The Southern kitchen is a place where bacon's sizzlin', grits are simmerin', collards are stewin', fried chicken is poppin', and pecan pie is coolin'.

"Dining with one's friends and beloved family is certainly one of life's primal and most innocent delights, one that is both soul-satisfying and eternal." - Julia Child

DINING ROOM IN THE HOME OF FRANKIE AND BUCK LIMEHOUSE AT AIRY HALL PLANTATION IN SOUTH CAROLINA.

A memorable Southern meal is just as much about the journey as the destination. Sunday suppers don't have to have a set time. They can take place after a lazy afternoon spent fishing on the river, after church, after a game of golf, or a day at the beach. The key to Sunday supper is that it brings family and friends together over food prepared with a whole lot of love and many times, cherished family recipes.

Long before we had cell phones, laptops, and walls of wired components, we had family suppers, we had conversation, and porches. The porch is where folks shelled peas, and snapped green beans in preparation for the family meal. With a bowl between her knees, my grandma would pull the string down the back of the pod and open it to loosen the peas inside. This old familiar act and the recipe from a loved one can help fill the void left after they are no longer with us. She had boxes filled with recipes written on the back of church bulletins, grocery store receipts, bank deposit slips, but mostly little 3 x 5 cards. Tattered and yellowed with age, little newspaper clippings were taped to these cards. Some are handwritten in her flowery script. All are now treasured keepsakes that connect us to her and memories of her Sunday suppers. If the card was heavily

KATHY ANDERSON

splattered, we knew the recipe would be a good one.

She always served her Sweet Potato Cornbread and her handmade biscuits, both slathered in farm-fresh butter. She mixed her biscuits in a big wooden bowl that always sat on the counter, using only her hands. Flour would be flying all over the place as she calmly went about the task. Just anticipating that first piece, hot and dripping with butter, was the best!

"The sun looks down on nothing so good as a household laughing together over a meal." C.S. Lewis

When autumn winds start to blow and that first chill of fall is in the air, it's time for a delicious Crown Pork Roast with Apple Stuffing. Serve with Sweet Potato Cornbread, Creamy Corn Pudding and this wonderful Citrus and Roasted Beet Salad.

There's no better way to start than with some of these steamed clams fresh from the waters of Beaufort County. Well, if you're not from here - bless your heart.

SWEET POTATO CORNBREAD

A favorite bread to serve with seafood, soups, gumbos and Brunswick stew

1 ¼ pounds red-skinned sweet potatoes (yams)

4 large eggs

1 ½ cups buttermilk

2 ⅓ cups yellow cornmeal

1 cup all-purpose flour

½ cup sugar

1 tablespoon baking powder

1½ teaspoons salt

½ teaspoon baking soda

¼ teaspoon ground ginger

½ cup chilled unsalted butter, cut into ½-inch pieces

Preheat oven to 375 degrees. Butter a 9x9x2-inch baking pan. Pierce sweet potatoes in several places. Microwave on high until tender, turning once, about 12 minutes. Cut open and cool. Mash enough

potatoes to yield 1 cup packed down. Place 1 cup mashed potatoes into a large mixing bowl. Whisk in eggs and buttermilk.

Blend cornmeal and next 6 ingredients in a processor. Add butter and blend until mixture resembles coarse meal. Add to egg mixture. Stir just until blended well. Pour into a prepared pan.

Place in the oven and bake until cornbread is a deep golden brown on top and a tester inserted into the center comes out clean, about 45 minutes. Cool in pan on a rack and serve with farm-fresh butter.

APPLE TART WITH SALTED CARAMEL

Serves 12

14-ounce package puff pastry, defrosted in fridge overnight

3 to 4 medium apples

2 tablespoons granulated sugar

2 tablespoons unsalted butter, cold and cut into small bits

¼ cup granulated sugar

2 tablespoons unsalted butter

¼ teaspoon flaky sea salt

2 tablespoons heavy cream

Heat oven to 400ºF. Line a rimmed baking sheet or jelly roll pan with parchment paper. A smaller pan will make a thicker

tart and you might need fewer apples.

Lightly flour your counter and lay out your pastry. Flour the top and gently roll it until it fits inside your baking sheet, and transfer it there. Roll it out to the size you need for your pan.

Peel apples and cut them in half top-to-bottom. Remove cores and stems with a paring knife. Slice apple halves crosswise as thinly as you can with a knife or mandolin. Leave a ½-inch border and fan the apples around the tart, slightly overlapping each slice. Each apple should overlap the one before so that only about ¾ inch of the previous apple will be visible. Sprinkle apples evenly with the first two tablespoons of sugar, then dot with two tablespoons butter. Bake for 30 minutes until edges are brown. Apples should feel soft to the touch.

Make glaze in a small saucepan over medium-high heat. Melt ¼ cup sugar and stir for about 3 minutes until liquefied and a nice copper color. Remove from heat and add sea salt and butter and stir until incorporated. Add heavy cream and return to the stove. Cook while stirring until you have a caramel syrup, about another 2 minutes. Set aside. Rewarm it to thin the caramel before brushing it over the tart.

Brush the entire tart, even the pastry. Return to the oven for 5 minutes until the glaze is bubbly. Cool and cut into slices. Serve with a scoop of French vanilla ice cream. Yum!

STEAMED CLAMS

Recipe inspired by Matthew Roher of Sea Pines, Hilton Head, South Carolina. Charting the tides, squinting in search of tiny clam holes and breaking a fingernail or two while digging in the sand is among the simpler summer pleasures of living by the sea. But cooking up a great appetizer for a party on the deck makes the day's labor one of the most gratifying rewards of a lazy summer afternoon.

Serves: 10-12 appetizer portions

5 dozen clams

⅓ cup olive oil

4-5 cloves garlic, minced

4 ounces Italian sausage, cut into a small dice

1 tablespoons dried oregano

1 teaspoon fennel seeds

Salt and freshly ground black pepper

1 ½ cups vermouth

Juice of ½ lemon

Scrub and rinse clams under cold running water to get rid of any sand. Heat oil in a large stockpot over high heat. Add garlic and sausage and cook, stirring constantly, for 5 minutes. Add oregano, fennel seeds, salt, and pepper and cook for another minute.
Pour vermouth and lemon juice into the pot and then add clams. Cover pot tightly. Cook until they open and throw out any that do not. Ladle clams into shallow bowls and serve with crunchy bread.

chloeschache@gmail.co

CROWN PORK ROAST WITH APPLE STUFFING

10 pounds pork rib roast

   (about 12 to 14 ribs), Frenched

1 bunch thyme, leaves only

1 small bunch fresh sage, leaves only

2 cloves garlic, minced

Kosher salt and freshly ground black pepper

1 cup extra-virgin olive oil

For stuffing:

3 tablespoons extra virgin olive oil

3 cloves garlic, peeled and crushed

4 leaves fresh sage

4 sprigs fresh thyme

2 large onions, diced small

Kosher salt and freshly ground black pepper

3 Granny Smith apples, cored and cut into small wedges

1½ cups pecans, chopped

2 large eggs, lightly beaten

¾ cup heavy cream

1½ cups chicken stock

5 cups sourdough bread, crusts removed and torn into small

   pieces

½ cup flat-leaf parsley, chopped

Extra-virgin olive oil for drizzling over stuffing

For pan sauce:

1½ cups water

¼ cup red-currant or apple jelly

Preheat oven to 375ºF. Set rack on the bottom third of the oven to give it plenty of room.

In a small bowl, or with a mortar and pestle, combine thyme, sage, garlic and salt and pepper, to taste. Mash together, breaking up herbs and garlic. Add oil and combine using the pestle.

To French, clean the meat off the ends of the bones with a boning knife. Make a small cut into the meat in between each rib so you can easily wrap the roast into a circle. Rub the pork all over with the herb mixture. With the ribs on the outside, wrap the roast into a circle so the ends meet and secure with kitchen twine. Note: If you are doing this by yourself, use a skewer to help hold the roast's shape while you wrap the twine.

Place in a roasting pan. Add any scraps into the bottom of the pan. Sprinkle roast inside and out with salt and pepper. Set aside to bring the pork to room temperature prior to cooking.

Stuffing: Preheat oven to 400ºF. Heat large skillet over medium heat. Add olive oil, garlic, sage and thyme until the herbs crackle. Remove garlic, sage and thyme and discard. Add onions to pan and cook slowly over medium-low heat until caramelized, about 15 to 20 minutes. Season with salt and pepper. Transfer onions to a bowl. Add apple wedges and pecans to the skillet and gently sauté. Lightly toast the pecans and soften the apples, about 5 minutes.

In a medium-sized mixing bowl, whisk together the egg, cream and chicken stock. Add bread, caramelized onions, apple mixture and chopped parsley. Use a wooden spoon to mix the dressing until well combined. Season with salt and pepper and drizzle with olive oil.

Mound stuffing in cavity. Wrap tips of rib bones with foil to prevent burning. Roast pork in middle of oven, covering stuffing loosely with foil after 30 minutes, until an instant-read thermometer registers 155ºF when inserted 2 inches into center of meat. (do not allow it to touch the bone), 2¼ to 2¾ hours total.

Transfer roast to a carving board and let stand, loosely covered with foil, 15 to 20 minutes. Temperature will rise to 160ºF and meat will be slightly pink.

Pan Sauce: Skim fat from pan dripping. Straddle pan across 2 burners and add water, then deglaze pan by boiling over high heat, stirring and scraping up brown bits. Pour through a fine sieve into a saucepan and discard solids.

Add the red-currant or apple jelly and simmer. Whisk and skim off any fat that rises, until jelly is melted, about 4 minutes. Season with salt and pepper. Pour into a gravy boat and serve with the roast. Remove foil from roast and carve into chops by cutting between ribs.

CREAMY CORN PUDDING

Inspired by a visit to The Blue Willow Inn, Social Circle, Georgia

Serves 6-8

1 tablespoon unsalted butter, softened

1 ½ cups fresh or frozen corn

2 scallions, trimmed and minced

½ red bell pepper, cored, seeded, and diced

1 tablespoon yellow cornmeal

2 tablespoons sugar

2 teaspoons chopped fresh basil

2 teaspoons salt

freshly ground black pepper

1 cup half-and-half

5 large eggs, beaten

1 cup sharp cheddar cheese, grated

Preheat oven to 350 degrees. Rub the butter on the bottom and side of a 3-quart soufflé dish or deep casserole dish.

Combine the corn, scallions, red bell pepper, cornmeal, sugar, basil, salt and pepper in a large bowl and stir to mix.

Whisk the half-and-half and eggs together in a separate bowl. Stir in the cheese. Mix the egg mixture with the corn mixture, and stir to combine. Pour the mixture into prepared soufflé dish and bake 55 minutes to 1 hour or until puffy and light golden brown. The pudding should be very moist and soft in the center.

Remove from the oven and allow to stand at room temperature for 10 minutes before serving.

SEARED AHI TUNA SALAD

An elegant, very easy way to serve this meaty fish. Everyone enjoys this salad but in cooler weather, simply serve on a bed of sautéed spinach over grits. Then sprinkle a little dressing on top.

Serves 4

Sesame Ginger Dressing:

½ cup extra virgin olive oil

¼ cup fresh lime juice

¼ cup orange juice

2 tablespoons soy sauce

2 tablespoons Oriental sesame oil

1 teaspoon rice vinegar

1 tablespoon brown sugar

1 tablespoon minced fresh ginger

4 fresh ahi tuna steaks

6 tablespoons sesame seeds

Mixed greens and arugula

Wonton strips

slivered almonds, toasted for garnish

Whisk olive oil, lime juice, orange juice, soy sauce, sesame oil, rice vinegar, brown sugar, and ginger together in a small bowl. Season with salt and pepper.

Sprinkle fish with salt and pepper. Dip fish into sesame seeds, coating on all sides and pressing fish to make seeds adhere. Heat skillet on high and sear fish until fish is nicely browned on all sides. Turn heat to medium and cook to your desired degree of doneness. This is often served very rare. Transfer fish to a cutting board.

Toss lettuce with dressing and mound on 4 plates. Thinly slice fish and arrange slices overlapping on lettuce. Garnish with wonton strips and slivered almonds.

LINDSAY GOODWIN

NANCY RICKER RHETT

CURRIED CHICKEN SALAD

The secret here is the addition of the wine in which the raisins are simmered. It thins the mayonnaise into a light, delicate curry sauce.
Serves 6-8

3 pounds boneless, skinless chicken breasts, poached until
   tender and cooled

2 celery ribs, chopped

2 Granny Smith apples, cut into small pieces

¾ cup golden raisins

1 cup dry white wine

2 tablespoons fresh lime juice

2 tablespoons ground ginger

2-3 tablespoons curry powder

1 ½ cups good mayonnaise

Kosher salt and freshly ground black pepper

Shred cooked chicken, removing and discarding any tough pieces. Toss the chicken, celery, and apples together in a bowl and set aside. Place raisins and wine in a small saucepan. Heat to boiling over medium-high heat. Reduce the heat and simmer for 4 minutes. Add raisins and liquid to the chicken and toss to thoroughly combine. Add lime juice, ginger, and curry powder and toss again. Stir in enough mayonnaise to bind the salad and season again with salt. Transfer to a serving dish and garnish with apple slices. Place in refrigerator to chill before serving.

A TIP ON POACHING CHICKEN BREASTS

This process will assure you of having tender, sweet chicken for your salads every time. Never, ever boil a chicken! It only toughens the meat.
Fill a large saucepan with water and add several onion slices, chopped celery, parsley, salt, and pepper and finally some dry vermouth. Then add the chicken breasts. Heat water just until it is about to boil, then turn it down to the very lowest temperature. Let this little bit of heat cook the meat and you will have the most moist and tender chicken ever.

COBB SALAD WITH GREEN GODDESS DRESSING

Summertime often calls for lighter fare as local farm stands overflow with the bounty of the land. This is a salad for hammocks and sunlight and having just one more bite.
Serves 8

Several handfuls of mixed greens

8 hard-cooked eggs, quartered

8 slices bacon, cooked and chopped

5 cups roasted chicken

3 cups honey-roasted deli ham, sliced thin

1 pint grape tomatoes

3 avocados, chopped

1 English cucumber, sliced thin

1 (8-ounce) container feta cheese, crumbled

Place mixed greens on a large platter. Arrange hard boiled eggs, bacon, tomatoes, avocados, cucumber, chicken, ham and feta cheese on the lettuce. Serve with Green Goddess Dressing on the side.

Green Goddess Dressing

You'll find all kinds of uses for this dressing from sandwiches to heirloom tomatoes over bibb lettuce, or simply stirred into a bowl of freshly sliced cucumbers and tomatoes.

1 cup mayonnaise

1 cup fresh basil leaves, chopped

1 cup sweet onion, chopped fine

¼ cup lemon juice, freshly squeezed

2 cloves garlic, minced

1 teaspoon each salt and freshly ground black pepper

1 cup sour cream

Blend together the mayonnaise, onions, basil, lemon juice, garlic, and salt and pepper. Add the sour cream and process just until blended. Refrigerate until ready to use.

GREEN PEA AND PROSCIUTTO SALAD

Sweet, chubby peapods on the vine are a beautiful sight each spring, but did you realize they are little vitamin powerhouses and packed with protein?
Serves 4-6

1 tablespoon fresh lemon juice

½ teaspoon Dijon mustard

3 tablespoons olive oil

kosher salt and freshly ground black pepper

1 ¼ cups shelled fresh green peas, or frozen peas thawed

3 cups sugar snap peas, trimmed

6 cups spinach or arugula

¼ pound prosciutto, thinly sliced

Parmigiano-Reggiano, shaved thin

Whisk lemon juice and mustard in a large bowl. Gradually add oil, whisking constantly until emulsified. Season with salt and pepper. Blanch green peas and sugar snap peas in a large stockpot of boiling salted water until crisp-tender, about 2-3 minutes. Immediately transfer to a bowl of ice water and stir peas around until cold. This will stop the cooking process and set their color.
Add peas, sugar snap peas, and arugula or spinach to a bowl with vinaigrette and toss until well coated. Season with salt and pepper.
Arrange salad on a platter and top with prosciutto and shaved Parmigiano-Reggiano.

Shannon Smith

TYLER'S BANANAS FOSTER

Executive Chef Tyler Slade, 10 Market, Beaufort, South Carolina
For the sauce, we recommend using whole spices to obtain the best flavors.

¼ cup wild honey

3 bay leaves

12 black peppercorns

5 green cardamom pods

6 allspice

6 cloves

1 cup orange juice

¾ cup brown sugar

1 cup dark rum

¼ cup banana liqueur or more rum

In a saucepan, heat honey and spices until mixture is bubbling. Add the rest of the ingredients and cook over medium-high heat until liquid is reduced by half. Strain sauce.

Slice 1 banana and sprinkle with sugar. Cook in a small sauté pan for 30 seconds. Add 2 ounces of Foster sauce and 1 tablespoon butter. Cook until butter is incorporated. Use one banana per serving. Serve over ice cream of your choice.

Chef Tyler Slade throwing cinnamon into the fire as he prepares to cook Bananas Foster.

SC&G Lifestyle

Tablescape by Susan Mason of Savannah, Georgia.

very thick. Remove from heat, and stir in the butter, vanilla extract, and almond extract. Allow the custard to cool to room temperature, and then chill in the refrigerator.

Place chilled whipping cream into a bowl, and beat with a hand-held mixer until the cream just begins to form peaks. Add the powdered sugar and beat until the cream forms stiff peaks. Refrigerate whipped cream until it is time to assemble the trifle.

To assemble the trifle, cut the pound cake into ½-inch slices. Wash the strawberries, cut off the tops and cut into thin slices. In a trifle bowl, place one layer of pound cake on the bottom and sprinkle with sherry. Top the pound cake with a layer of strawberries, then a layer of custard, followed by a layer of whipped cream. Repeat. Finish the trifle with a topping of whipped cream and garnish with fresh mint.

CAROLINA TRIFLE

Adapted from Susan Mason

Serves 8 to 10

Every host and hostess in the South has to have a trifle recipe in his or her repertoire. It is a beautiful statement dessert that can be put together quickly.

For the custard:

⅔ cup sugar

2 tablespoons cornstarch

¼ teaspoon salt

2 cups whole milk

4 egg yolks

2 tablespoons unsalted butter

1 teaspoon vanilla extract

1 teaspoon almond extract

1 pint heavy whipping cream

Powdered sugar, to taste

1 large pound cake

2 pints strawberries

Dry sherry

Fresh mint

In a small saucepan, combine sugar, cornstarch, salt, and milk. Heat over medium heat, stirring constantly until the mixture becomes thick and bubbly, about, 7 minutes. Remove from heat and allow to cool for 2 minutes.

Separate the eggs and place the yolks in a small bowl. Slowly pour half of the milk mixture into the eggs while whisking constantly. Once the mixture is tempered, add the remaining milk and return the mixture to the saucepan. Heat for 2 minutes over low heat, until the mixture is

Holidays

All is Merry and Bright

Chapter Ten

The raw, damp chill of the ocean is everywhere; piercing winds from offshore remind us of what

it must have been like in early colonial America when islanders were sent scurrying back to their

houses to snuggle around eighteenth-century coal-burning fireplaces.

Local oystermen, wearing their whiteboots, head out to the rugged oyster banks at dawn each day

as perfect testimony to the Lowcountry's ongoing reliance upon the bounty of the sea. Salt-misted

Brussels sprouts still on the stalk, turnips, kale and spinach signal the winter farm season.

DESIGNED BY SEBRELL SMITH.

A mid the hustle of the holidays, there is a moment when Christmas happens. It may be the sounds of carolers in the neighborhood that suddenly lifts the heart, the arrival home of a loved one from far away, or the jingle of bells and the twinkle of lights seen and heard on city streets. Or sometimes it's the simple act of lifting the wreath onto the front door. Scents of sweet cedar and fresh cut magnolia leaves bring a rush of memories of Christmas past.

Home is never more dear to us than during this season of joy and reflection. Though certain traditions, stockings hung on the mantel in a certain order, a special angel that must be set atop the tree, may be unchangeable, there are many touches open to pure invention. All is merry and bright as decorations are ready for Christmas. No other holiday connects us so deeply to our past through beloved family treasures – and offers such promise to build our own collections and traditions. Whether our ornaments and decorations are inherited or bought, memories are what they display each year among the greenery.

Whispers of White

Along the towns and villages of the coastal South, snowflakes are a rare sight. However, with a little imagination, you can assemble a winter wonderland in your own home. Set the scene in front of your fireplace with hot cocoa and marshmallows and hues of soft and serene crème and white with just touches of gold accents.

Winter is the time for comfort, for good food, friends, family, and warmth, for the touch of a loving hand and a talk beside a glowing fire; it is a time for home.

CHEWY GINGERBREAD COOKIES WITH ORANGE GLAZE

Makes 12 cookies

½ cup unsalted butter, softened

½ cup firmly packed dark brown sugar

1 tablespoon orange zest

1 teaspoon orange extract

1 large egg

¼ cup blackstrap molasses

¼ cup honey

3 cups all-purpose flour

2 teaspoons ground cinnamon

1 ½ teaspoons ground ginger

½ teaspoon ground allspice

½ teaspoon baking soda

½ teaspoon kosher salt

¼ teaspoon ground cloves

¼ teaspoon baking powder

¼ teaspoon ground cardamom

Preheat oven to 350 degrees. Line baking sheets with parchment paper. In a large bowl, beat butter, brown sugar, orange zest, and orange extract with a mixer at medium speed until creamy, 3 to 4 minutes, stopping to scrape sides of bowl. Add egg, beating well. Beat in molasses and honey.

In a medium bowl, whisk together flour, cinnamon, ginger, allspice, baking soda, salt, cloves, baking powder, and cardamom. With mixer on low speed, gradually add flour mixture to butter mixture, beating until well combined.
On a lightly floured surface, roll dough to ⅓ inch thickness. Using desired cutters, cut dough, rerolling scraps as necessary. Place on prepared pans.
Bake until edges are lightly browned, 10 to 14 minutes, rotating pans halfway through baking. Let cool on pans for 2 minutes. Remove from pans, and let cool completely on wire racks. Dip top side of

cookies in Orange Glaze, and place on a sheet of parchment paper, glaze side up. Let stand until set, about 30 minutes. Garnish with cinnamon sugar, if desired.

Orange Glaze

2-3 cups confectioners' sugar, sifted

¼ cup fresh orange juice

1 teaspoon orange extract

In a medium bowl, whisk together 3 cups confectioners' sugar, orange juice, and orange extract until smooth. Add remaining 1 cup confectioners' sugar to reach desired consistency, if necessary. The thinner the glaze, the more it will harden on the cookie.

HOMEMADE HOT COCOA

Serves 3

Making hot cocoa from scratch, while quite simple, is one of winter's more decadent pastimes. No mix can ever compare with the luxury and richness of this home blend. A cup may be made even more potable by lacing it with a jigger of any number of cordials such as Grand Marnier, Vandermint, or raspberry Chambord.

⅓ cup brewed coffee

1 ounce unsweetened chocolate

1 tablespoon unsweetened cocoa powder

5 tablespoons sugar

1 ½ cups milk

1 cup half-and-half

¼ teaspoon almond extract

Combine the coffee, chocolate, cocoa, and sugar in a small saucepan. Heat over medium heat, stirring frequently, until the chocolate is melted and the sugar dissolved. Stir in the milk, half-and-half, and almond extract. Heat until piping hot, but not boiling. Pour the mixture into a blender and blend until light and frothy. Pour into mugs and serve at once.

SC&G Lifestyle

ANGELA TROTTA THOMAS

Memories of Christmas Past Come Alive Through the Art of Angela Trotta Thomas

As I raced for the Christmas presents under the tree, I scurried through the dining room where Dad had set up a shiny 1957 Santa Fe Lionel train. It clicked around an oval track, had smoke coming out of its smokestack and the whistle blew as it approached a little village made up of figurines ice skating on a pond and strolling through tiny streets. These miniature figures inhabited the town. Along the track were an oversized metal tunnel, a bridge and several signal towers. Dad was a good teacher: "Not too fast around the curves, go slowly through the tunnel and over the bridges, and slow down when you get to the settlement."

Since that morning, it's never seemed like Christmas without the clickety-click and whistle of a train. Each of my three children learned to take the throttle and run the train at least once every year. If ever I suggested not bothering to set it up, there would be groans, "You have to!" The tradition of going into the attic to find the boxes, the sounds of the cars going clickety-click, the nasal horn blowing as it rounded the bend, and smells of oil and smoke from the smokestack, became as much a part of the holiday as our stockings, nativity scenes and sugar cookies. I believe no matter how old we are, there will forever be magic when the train appears each year.

ANGELA TROTTA THOMAS

FEAST OF SEVEN FISHES PIRLOU On Carolina Gold Rice

Mrs. Samuel G. Stoney, Charleston, S.C., December 1901 from *The Carolina Rice Cookbook*, compiled by Mrs. Samuel G. Stoney reprinted in facsimile in *The Carolina Rice Kitchen* by Karen Hess

So much of my cooking is informed by Carolina Gold rice culture. Whether "pilou," "perlou," or "perlo" this is a quintessential Carolina rice dish, and a delicious way of remembering our shared history. The method for the rice is foolproof and consistent - many thanks to "Hoppin' John" Taylor for sharing this from Vertamae Grosvenor. Grosvenor was a Hampton County native who put "Geechee" on the world map beginning in 1970 with a book "The Travel Notes of a Geechee Girl," often described as an autobiographical cookbook. Vertamae's books were to the Gullah culture what Jonathan Green's paintings are today. They brought Gullah Geechee to the forefront with reckless abandon.

In Italy, it is not infrequent for Christmas Eve to be celebrated with the famous Feast of Seven Fishes, or Festa dei Sette Pesci.

Rice

  1 cup rice

  1 ¾ cups water

  pinch salt

  1 bay leaf

Do not rinse the rice. Combine rice, water, salt and bay leaf in a medium pot. Bring to a boil, reduce heat to a simmer and cover. Cook for 13 minutes. Turn off the heat and rest for 10 minutes. DO NOT LIFT THE LID TO LOOK. When finished, fluff with a fork. Allow to cool.

Heat a nonstick skillet to medium high. Add oil, then place a half cup of cooked rice in the skillet. Using a heat-proof silicone spatula, mash the rice into a disc. Allow to cook undisturbed until rice has browned slightly and become crispy around the edges. Flip and continue cooking until both sides are browned and crispy. Remove from heat and repeat, allowing one disc for each guest.

Note: this is also a great vehicle for leftover rice. If using leftover rice, follow the same process but add a teaspoon water to refresh the rice as it cooks in the skillet.

For the Seven Fishes

8 South Carolina shrimp, peeled and deveined. (Head on shrimp not only make for a dramatic presentation but are also delicious if you're so inclined.)

8 clams, oysters or sweetwater mussels

4 pieces of octopus, canned or cooked and frozen

½ pound lump crab

8 - 2 oz. portions of grouper filet

2 small lobster tails, split and deveined, shell on

Any other local, fresh fish or shellfish such as sheepshead

Good quality extra virgin olive oil

Salt and pepper

White wine

This is really more of a process than a recipe per se, but the long and short of it is that you're searing or grilling all the seafood, holding it and warming it briefly before presenting in the finished dish.

Bring a large non-stick or cast iron skillet to medium high heat. Season any fish or shellfish liberally with salt and pepper. Add a drizzle of cooking oil to the skillet and begin laying in the assorted seafood. Allow to cook until the edges have browned and the meat releases from the pan freely. Turn and repeat for 3 minutes, then remove to a sheet tray. Any bi-valves such as clams, mussels or oysters will require a generous splash of wine, stock or beer to aid in getting them open, so cook separately just until they barely open.

Broth

  1 cup white wine

  1 cup shrimp stock or good quality clam juice

  pinch of saffron threads

  3 tablespoons unsalted butter

  Sliced cherry tomatoes

Sliced mild chiles, such as padron, shishito or fresno

Salt and pepper to taste

Combine the first three ingredients and reduce by half over a medium flame. Remove from heat and whisk in butter, tomatoes and chiles - residual heat will warm them through without hammering them. Season to taste.

For the Presentation: Pre-heat your oven to 350 degrees. Add the sheet tray of cooked fish. Line up 4 bowls for plating, slide a warm disc of rice into each. Remove the fish from the oven and place on top of the rice discs, dividing into 4 equal portions. Ladle or spoon the tomato / chile / saffron broth over each.

Chef Forrest Parker likes to add toasted benne seed and a modicum of microgreens or foraged chainey briar to the dish for color and flair.

Food is the Soul of the Gathering

Whatever your region, look for the best local ingredients. I have searched my own family past for cherished taste memories and my enthusiasm for the recipes in this chapter is boundless.

The Feast of the Seven Fishes is an old Christmas Eve tradition. Our recipe is the inspiration of Chef Forrest Parker of Charleston. If your family loves seafood, they surely will be excited with this traditional dish.

MEDITERRANEAN STYLE SNAPPER AL CARTOCCIO

This easy recipe is quick enough for a holiday weeknight dinner, but delicious enough for a dinner party! If you can't find snapper, any thin, mild white fish will work. Cooking the fish in a foil parcel keeps the fish moist and steams the vegetables. When vegetables are all at the peak of freshness, this dish soars. This recipe is courtesy of Chef Kim Baretta of Hilton Head Island. **Serves 4**

4 5-ounce snapper fillets

3 tablespoons extra virgin olive oil

2 teaspoons dried oregano

2 teaspoons fresh chopped flat leaf parsley

2 garlic cloves, peeled and halved

⅛ teaspoon salt

⅛ teaspoon pepper

1 medium sized red onion, cut in half and sliced thin

¼ pound cherry tomatoes, halved

3 tablespoons capers, drained and rinsed

12 black olives, pitted and halved

Toss fish in olive oil, oregano, parsley, garlic, salt, pepper. Cover base of baking tray with foil. Place a bed of onions on foil.

Lay fish on onions, skin side down. Sprinkle with cherry tomatoes, capers and olives Cover with foil and bake at 375 degrees for 20-25 minutes. Open foil carefully as steam will be very hot.

FAVORITE PECAN PIE

What makes this pie incredible and totally different from any other pecan pie if the addition of espresso powder and bittersweet chocolate. Not a lot, but just enough to keep the sugar from being the first, strongest, longest and most memorable flavor in the pie. I learned this little trick from Dorie Greenspan. In fact, in this pie, you can taste the pecans!

1 9-inch single crust, partially baked and cooled

¾ cup light corn syrup

½ cup light brown sugar

3 tablespoons unsalted butter, melted and cooled

3 large eggs, room temperature

2 teaspoons instant espresso powder

1 teaspoon pure vanilla extract

½ teaspoon ground cinnamon

¼ teaspoon salt

1½ cups pecan halves or piece

3 ounces bittersweet chocolate, coarsely chopped

Preheat oven to 425 degrees. Place pie plate on a baking sheet lined with a silicone mat or parchment.

Whisk corn syrup and brown sugar together until a smooth consistency. Whisk in the melted butter, then add the eggs one at a time, beating until you have a smooth, foamy mixture. Add espresso powder, vanilla, cinnamon and salt and give the batter a good mix. Rap the bowl against the counter a couple of times to pop any bubbles that might have formed, then stir in the pecans and chocolate. Pour the filling into the crust.

Bake pie for 15 minutes. Make a foil shield for the crust by cutting a 9-inch circle out of the center of an 11 or 12-inch square of foil. Lower temperature to 350 degrees. Place foil shield on top of the pie-crust. The filling will be exposed but the crust covered by the foil. Bake another 15 to 20 minutes until it has puffed and is browned and no longer jiggles when tapped. Transfer pie plate to a rack and cool.

Note: If you prefer a great plain pecan pie, omit the cinnamon, espresso and chocolate. If you want a sweeter pie, increase the amount of corn syrup to 1 cup. Serves 8 to 10.

GREEK INSPIRED ROLLED COLLARD GREENS

Yields 2 dozen stuffed leaves

1 large bunch collard greens

¼ cup extra virgin olive oil

1 large red onion, finely chopped

4 cloves garlic, minced

Kosher salt to taste

1 teaspoon sugar

¾ cup basmati rice, rinsed well in several changes of water

¼ cup lightly toasted pine nuts

1 (14 ounce) can chopped tomatoes, drained (retain juice)

¼ cup dark raisins

¾ teaspoon cinnamon

¾ teaspoon allspice

½ teaspoon freshly ground black pepper

1 ¼ cups water

2 tablespoons chopped fresh mint

Juice of 1 lemon

Fill a bowl with ice water. Bring a large stockpot of water to a boil while you stem the collard greens, leaving the leaves intact. Once boiling, salt the water and add the leaves in batches. Blanch 2 minutes and plunge into the ice water. Drain and squeeze out excess water and set aside.

Heat 2 tablespoons of the oil over medium heat in a large skillet and add the onion. Once tender, add the garlic, salt and sugar. Add the rice and pine nuts and stir until the rice is coated.

Stir in the tomatoes, raisins, cinnamon, allspice, salt and pepper. Bring to a boil and reduce heat. Simmer until all liquid is absorbed. Remove from heat and cool down. Stir in the mint.

Heat oil in a large saucepan. To fill the leaves, place them on your work surface, vein side up and the stem end facing you. Add about 1 level tablespoon of filling on the bottom center of each leaf. Fold the sides over and roll up tightly, tucking the sides as you go. Place seam side down in the pan, fitting the stuffed leaves in snug layers. Drizzle with remaining olive oil, and pour on the lemon juice. Barely cover with water.

Put a plate over the leaves to weigh them down during cooking so they will not open. Simmer 45 minutes. Carefully remove each leaf from the pan with a slotted spoon. Allow to drain. Serve warm or cold.

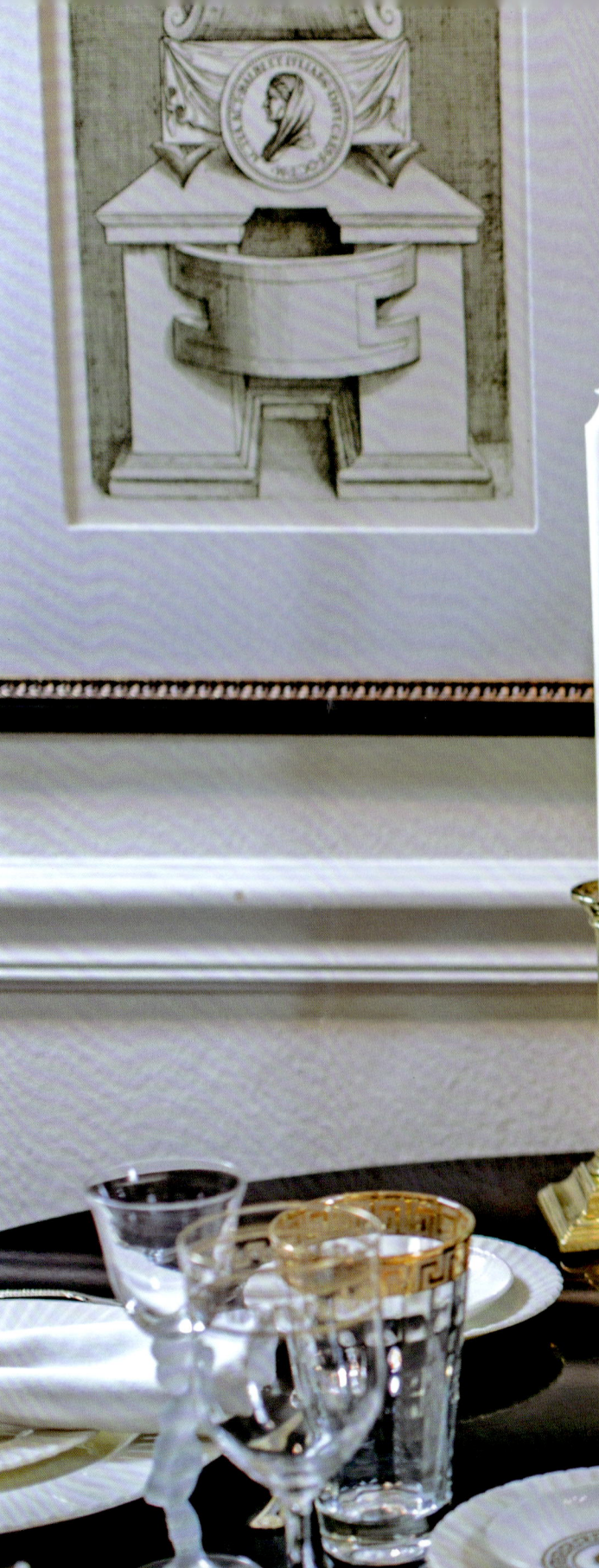

A Greek Inspired New Year's Dinner

The Allure of the Black and White Palette

Shortly after Christmas Day, I become tired of the constant coupling of red and green. Gardening catalogs start pouring in and I become anxious for the freshness of spring. The dark winter skies come early in the evening and have me longing for the bright light and green colors that come with the change of seasons.

The gold vase in the center of the table was once owned by Versace. It is filled with grape leaves and grapes pushed into floral foam.

Gold-rimmed glassware, candlesticks and napkin rings formalize the gaiety of the centerpiece.

The table is filled with decorative appointments such as candlesticks made to look like brass columns. The white Greek statues are Dionyus Baschus, Greek Gods of Wine and Joy, and Demeter Ceres, the Goddess of Harvest. Bright color will be absent for now, but textures fill the void.

Our New Year's table is set with cream china in a gold Greek key pattern, mini butter plates decorated with the images of Greek gods, silverware with Greek emblems, and 24 karat gold Greek god napkin rings with linen napkins embossed with Greek key designs.

Lovely glassware also carries the Greek key design along with antique Bacchus stemware used for champagne.

Special Thanks

The Family

My most heartfelt appreciation and thank you goes to my dear friend, designer Beth Blalock, whose taste and talents soar across the pages of this book. May her table designs and ideas fuel your desire to create a little magic when entertaining friends and loved ones. She is a champion of Southern hospitality, a true daughter of the South with endless charm and a boundless love for people and the art of entertaining. And to her daughter, Ashley Blalock, we give a round of applause for the many wonderful photographs of her mother's work that grace these pages. In her varied arsenal of skills, there is the fine art of baking which brings out the child in each one of us when we view her Winter Wonderland.

We thank Mike Cook of Hilton Head Island for his travels to Montefalco, Italy where he tasted the deliciousness of the very special dishes he was served while visiting there. He then gathered the recipes, prepared them for us and served them at his home in the Lowcountry.

To the joys of my heart, my husband, children, and grandchildren, a very special thank you for your thoughtfulness, love and patience throughout the duration of this project.

The paintings of 28 artists shine through the pages of *Southern Traditions* contributing the timeless beauty of some of the South's finest artwork. We acknowledge

LEFT TO RIGHT: Elizabeth, Jada, Pat, George, Cloide, Andrew, Ava, Margaret, Percy & Simon.

the chefs, the farmers, oystermen, shrimpers and all the watermen responsible for our way of life. Much praise to each and every one of the spirited men and women who quietly go about their daily lives preserving the best of this great region. Thank you all for contributing to the cultural collective we celebrate and explore.

A most special thanks to the late John Carroll Doyle and Gallery Director Angela Stump for our cover painting, *Conference on Church Street*, oil on canvas, copyright 2001. The John C. Doyle Art Gallery is located at 125 Church Street in historic Charleston.

LINDSAY GOODWIN

Artists' Biographies

Kathy Anderson

"My passion for painting is rooted in my garden. I strive to translate my excitement about the experience of growth, light, and translucent colors from the earth to my canvas." Anderson has received many top awards and is regularly invited to be a guest artist in prestigious national shows. Kathy is an elected Artist Member of the Salmagundi Club and the National Arts Club in New York City. In the Lowcountry, Kathy's work is exhibited at Horton Hayes Fine Arts in Charleston. She resides in Connecticut with her husband, John Anderson.

Ashley Blalock

Ashley is a graduate of SCAD, Savannah, Georgia with a degree in metals and jewelry, an entrepreneur with many talents. A gifted photographer as well as an accomplished designer of fine jewelry, Ashley created ALB Designs in 2008, her own brand specializing in elegant handcrafted jewelry.

Andrew Branning

Photographer and publisher of the *Shrimp, Collards and Grits* series of Southern lifestyle books, and publisher of the regional magazine SC&G Lifestyle. Andrew is a native of Beaufort, South Carolina and is well known for his large format black and white prints depicting the timeless beauty of the Lowcountry. He is a visionary in his efforts to preserve the wild and scenic areas of the Lowcountry for future generations. www.andrewbranning.com

Brian Brown

Abandoned gas stations, old churches and boarded-up corner stores litter Georgia's countryside and small towns. They tell the story of what once was. Brian Brown, a Georgia native, has made it his mission to photograph the "vanishing" buildings of Georgia – not just for the historical record but for the memories they evoke when we see them. vanishingsouthgeorgia.com

John Carroll Doyle – 1942-1914

He painted his passion for the Lowcountry into our very souls. "Although I had no formal education as a painter, Charleston, in its romantic light, was my first art teacher." – John Carroll Doyle

John Carroll Doyle Art Gallery is located at 125 Church Street, Charleston, South Carolina

Doug Corkern

"I'm recording my Lowcountry. That's what I feel that I'm doing. That's what I want to do. I love its people, its places and animals." His drawings are mostly pen and ink, sometimes splashed with watercolor revealing the simple sights we see in everyday life around Bluffton, Corkern's hometown. A graduate of Clemson University who arrived in Bluffton in 1960, met Charles Fraser, and helped design the Hilton Head look before retiring 13 years ago to the banks of Huger Cove on Bluffton's Lawrence Street.

Joan Eckhardt

Resides in Beaufort, S.C. where she shares her passion for the beauty and art of photography. Joan is a member of the Photography Club of Beaufort, www.photoclubbeaufort.com.

Sandy Dimke

Sandy spent almost 20 years in architectural photography in Connecticut with her husband, Russ before retiring to Beaufort. She concentrates on Fine Art Photography with a slight edge towards impressionism. Her artwork is currently on exhibit at the Brick Wall Gallery, 913 Bay St. in Beaufort.

Ted Ellis

Ted is an American artist and former environmental chemist best known for his African-American themed art and style which blend elements of folk art, naturalism and impressionism. A native of New Orleans, Louisiana, Ted is known to capture the essence of his subjects in all the glory of its rich cultural heritage. He is represented by the Stellers Gallery, Jacksonville, Florida.

West Fraser

West Fraser paints with light – the radiance of early morning, the glare of high noon, and the glow of day's end and the mystery of moonlight – to create brilliant works of color and form. West is a true son of the South, raised in Beaufort County, South Carolina.

Lindsay Goodwin

Lindsay is at the forefront of the art industry with awards and accolades from all of the country's leading art magazines, galleries and industry sources. She has a career most dare not dream. At the age of 33, she traveled throughout Europe studying architecture from the opulent opera houses down to the humblest of cobblestone cafes. She lives in California and is represented locally at Ella Walton Richardson Fine Art Gallery in Charleston, South Carolina.

Michael Harrell

He is rarely far from water where he depicts real people in real environments close to the water's edge with a depth of perception well beyond his years. From his native Florida panhandle to the Bahamas and up along the barrier islands of Georgia and South Carolina to Nantucket, Harrell moves quietly among the timeless moods of coastal living. Harrell is represented by The Red Piano Art Gallery, Bluffton, South Carolina.

Mark Kelvin Horton

Horton is especially interested in the effects of light and weather upon the landscape. He paints beyond a literal interpretation of a scene to portray nature in a way that reflects his own ideas and sensibilities while capturing the spirit, color and changing light of a place. His work may be viewed at Horton Hayes Fine Art, 30 State Street, Charleston, S.C.

Clark Hulings

The late Clark Hulings was an American realist painter born in Florida and raised in New Jersey. Clark is revered for his technique and venerated for capturing the essence of ancestral homelands. His subjects and composition are widely emulated, and he is recognized for his enormous impact on American realists, and especially Western artists.

Kendrick Mayes

For over 20 years Mayes has been the artist in residence at Airy Hall Plantation, deep in the ACE Basin, on the banks of the Ashepoo River. Step inside his white, circa-1920s clapboard house and you become immersed in his world of found and created objects. He shoots portraits, elements of farm life, landscape light and color and the two sports that take place at Airy Hall, fox hunting and polo.

Jim Palmer

Jim was born in Columbia, South Carolina and moved to Hilton Head Island in 1966, only the second artist to do so in the island's early years. Walter Greer had been the first. His paintings turned a Chamber of Commerce newsletter into a magazine called the Islander. Charles Fraser asked him to paint the Harbour Town Lighthouse – before there was a lighthouse. His many Lowcountry scenes now grace homes and businesses throughout the country. He is represented by The Red Piano Art Gallery, Bluffton, South Carolina.

Nancy Ricker Rhett

A genuine daughter of the South, Nancy is a native of Beaufort, South Carolina and an original in the very best sense of the word. Completely true to herself, she is a self-taught artist, historian and world traveler. She is equally at home with a shotgun in her hand quail hunting or in her studio painting Lowcountry scenes. See Nancy's work at the Rhett Gallery, Bay Street, Beaufort, South Carolina.

William Means Rhett III, and William Means Rhett, Jr.

They represent five generations of artists and many family connections. Nancy Rhett's relatives, who have been in Beaufort since the late 1600's, as land grant colonists, have names well known in the Lowcountry such as Elliott, Heyward, and Pinckney. Both Rhetts are descended from talented artists and interestingly, none of the Rhetts have had any formal artistic training.

James Richards

"You don't simply look at a James Richards painting, you look into it." So says Laurie Meyer, artist and co-owner of Meyer-Vogl Gallery, an art gallery in Charleston where James shows his work. "His paintings overflow with passion and energy and his subject matter evokes emotion. With layer upon layer of thick and thin paint, his intention is to create a spark and entertain the senses," says Meyer. James is a true son of the South, born and raised in rural Georgia.

Sandra Roper

Sandra grew up in South Carolina where she developed an appreciation for the history, architectural features, and beauty of Charleston. She is a graduate of the University of South Carolina in Studio Art. She is a member/owner of Lowcountry Artists Gallery, 148 East Bay Street in Charleston.

Murray Sease

A painter at the forefront of Bluffton's burgeoning art scene. In just 10 short years, Murray Sease has gone from picking up a paintbrush to showcasing her paintings at La Petite Galleria and in local art festivals. She started with painting homes for real estate clients, and her passion for painting blossomed from there. Bluffton inspires much of her art, the natural settings, the rich culture and the history of the Lowcountry are all themes for her paintngs.

Marilyn Simandle

Marilyn has always known that she would become an artist. Learning from her mother, a musician and painter, Marilyn started painting at the age of six. She received a B.A. Arts Degree from San Jose State University and went on to share her inspiration with the world. She believes the artist's role is to make the ordinary extraordinary and in the words of Robert Henri, "Perfection is the enemy of great art."

Shannon Smith

The Smith triplets, Shannon, Jennifer, and Tripp, all artists, are the children of renowned painter Betty Anglin Smith. Her oils are known for color, painterly brushwork, and capturing light in simple everyday scenes. It is her use of light that becomes the common thread in her work. Anglin Smith Fine Arts, 9 Queen Street, Charleston.

Sue Stewart

Sue is a graduate of the University of Georgia now living in Charleston. "Early in youth, I concluded that my surrounding environment was the most fascinating dimension that I might possibly control." Stewart Fine Art, 12 State Street, Charleston, South Carolina.

Joseph Sulkowski

Sulkowski was born in Pittsburgh, Pennsylvania and knew from the age of five that he would be an artist. His early skills in drawing and painting enabled him to begin a path toward fulfilling his passion.

His colors and shadows remind one of Rembrandt, his complex reds evoke Eugene Delacroix, and his viscous glowing surfaces suggest the great Dutch painter, Johannes Vermeer. He calls his style "poetic realism" because his canvases tell an immediate story and imply an entire world of sport beyond. Sulkowski's works clearly follow in the footsteps of the old masters of the 17th century such as Rembrandt, and Velazquez.

Angela Trotta Thomas

Angela is the only artist ever to be licensed by famed toy train manufacturer Lionel Trains Inc. and has held that honor for many years. Her work has been featured on the cover of numerous national magazines and catalog covers. Her toy train art has been exhibited in the Smithsonian and Everhart museums as well as others.

Jennifer Heyd Wharton

Jennifer is originally from Strafford, Pa. but lived for many years in Annapolis, Md. In 1997 she opened the highly acclaimed Troika Gallery in Easton, Md. and relocated to Beaufort, S.C. in 2014. "Making art, for me, is an expression of thanks and praise to God for the talent He has given me. My hope is to glorify Him through it."

MICHAEL HARRELL